Schools on Trial

Schools on Trial

The Trials of Democratic Comprehensives

Colin Fletcher, Maxine Caron
and Wyn Williams

Open University Press

Milton Keynes · Philadelphia

Open University Press
12 Cofferidge Close
Stony Stratford
Milton Keynes MK11 1BY. England
and
242 Cherry Street
Philadelphia, PA 19106, USA

First Published 1985

British Library Cataloguing in Publication Data

Fletcher, Colin
  Schools on trial: the trials of democratic
  comprehensives.
  1. Comprehensive high schools—England—
  Case studies
  I. Title   II. Caron, Maxine   III. Williams, Wyn
  373.2'5'0722   LA635

  ISBN 0-335-15022-5

Library of Congress Cataloging in Publication
No. LC 84-22728

Text Design by Clarke Williams

Typeset by Getset (BTS) Ltd, Eynsham, Oxford.
Printed in Great Britain by M. & A. Thomson Litho Limited,
East Kilbride, Scotland.

For Martin Galloway

and Debbie Meier

Contents

Contents

Acknowledgements

We wish to thank the following:

- The school heads for their correspondence.
- Sandra Hufton and Diana Palmer for their gifted running of the Research Office at Sutton Centre, 1976 to 1981.
- Carolyn Brown for her eagle eye on the text.
- The Cranfield Education Group: Eammon Cahill; Shirley Jones; Ken Mason; Jim Smith; Kate Stephens; Dina Thorpe and Roger Tingle, who thoroughly criticised the second draft.
- The three anonymous publishers' reviewers who pushed for many necessary improvements.
- The Fletcher family for giving up their dinner table and a host of other developmental rights.
- John Skelton, publisher, for being committed in spirit to a form with many flaws.
- Members of the Department of Social Policy, Cranfield, for their warm support of further drafting.
- Sue Isaac and Beryl Lodge for expertly typing, retyping, making further alterations. . .

And all the staff, pupils, parents, politicians and administrators who pioneered so much at Risinghill School, Summerhill Academy, Countesthorpe College and Sutton Centre.

Preface

Most of this book is taken up with telling what happened when four comprehensive schools were put on trial. By 'trial' we mean that each school experienced different kinds of courtroom dramas during which serious allegations and detailed investigations took place under a clause in the 1944 Education Act which says that 'pupils are to be educated in accordance with the wishes of their parents". We describe the schools' lives before their trials began. We reconstruct the rush of events during their fateful weeks and months and we seek to show what happened when the trials were over. Our first aim is to bring together new accounts of the trials at Risinghill School, Summerhill Academy, Countesthorpe College and Sutton Centre so that their experiences can be coolly and carefully understood. For, in their time, these trials were sensational. These secondary schools went through a period when the press and public buzzed with excitement over their difficulties. Some very important people made brief appearances, amongst them Margaret Thatcher, Shirley Williams, John Newsom and Ted Wragg. But sensationalism and profiles of public figures usually smother substance. So we try both to explain why the trials occurred and to say what lessons can be drawn from them. One of the lessons is that the schools had a vital ingredient in common.

These four schools gave distinctive answers to the question, What should a democratic comprehensive be like? All made great efforts to innovate, to be progressive and to be democratic. Each, too, ran foul of some parents and some local politicians. A tension emerged between becoming democratic comprehensives and being the focus of conflicts in the community at large. Consequently it is important to examine what these schools were in the process of becoming, as well as to record the traumas through which they went.

We have taken, then, two overlapping sets of questions, the first upon school trials and the second upon the nature of democratic comprehensives. Each purpose throws the other into sharp relief. Each provides much-needed answers for the other. These two sets of questions, when harnessed together, pull us from milestones in the recent past into the future of, and for, comprehensive education.

Introduction:

from critical incident to central issues

We first came together in November 1977 when a 'Nottinghamshire comprehensive' made news with headlines like:

'School for Swearing' (*Daily Mail*)
'Parents Cane the Cursing Classes' (*Daily Mirror*)
'"Four Letter Lesson" School Scandal' (*Sun*)

Trouble had been brewing for several weeks. Then a handful of parents had been angry over a lesson upon 'swearing' and had taken their complaint to a local councillor. The complaint went quickly and directly to the county council leader, and the head was summoned to be told that there would be an enquiry into the complaint and into further serious allegations which had since come to light. When the *Sun*, *Mirror*, *Daily Express* and *Daily Mail* descended one Monday morning the head and staff felt virtually damned and utterly defenceless.

The school, Sutton Centre, was much more than a school, as its name implies. It was, and is, a purpose-built community education centre right in the middle of a mining town. In September 1976 Colin Fletcher was appointed Senior Research Officer on a five-year project for Nottingham University's Adult Education Department. His brief was to record and write the story of Sutton Centre's development. When the crisis came a year later he asked for help; Wyn Williams and Maxine Caron joined him.

Wyn Williams was Senior Lecturer in Community Education at Nottinghamshire's Trent Polytechnic. He had worked on a Community Education Project in the early 1970s and taken an active interest in Sutton Centre through his students being on teaching practice there. Maxine Caron taught Liberal Studies at Trent Polytechnic and had a keen interest in the media. Between us we had a sufficient diversity of perspectives to prevent a regression into frenzied gossip. Colin Fletcher was concerned with 'community power' but already too closely identified with Sutton Centre to be able to interview the key hostile participants. He also had a year's worth of study materials which showed how the school had been developing before opposition to it had coalesced. Wyn Williams also had the school's history to hand and as an historian by training wanted as much precise, corroborated evidence as possible. Maxine Caron was soon to embark on an MA in Education and was more widely read than either of her collaborators. Furthermore the crisis was a media event; we desperately needed an archive and a thorough analysis of all that was happening.

Sutton Centre was on trial for six months. There were rumours, allegations, meetings, an inspection and a running battle in newspaper correspondence columns—all of which were tremendous stresses upon the school. Our first task was to write a cool account of how the trial had come about. This was to be an account which the serious national media could use. The aim was to broaden the issues from a swearing lesson to the question, What does community education mean in a secondary school? The account appeared, in part, in *New Society*[1] and was used as a source by *The Times Educational Supplement*.[2] The aim was not fully achieved because details about the early events were more publishable than was a discussion of what the school was trying to do. All the same the article did attract attention to the ethics of a local struggle and played a minor role in the call for 'fair play'.

We met every week, usually on a Friday, to collate what had been happening and to plan how to follow it up. There were decisions upon whom to interview and discussions upon where it was all leading. The central issue was that nobody knew which way the trial was going. The balance of forces altered week by week, and so too did the sense of likely outcome. Our concepts for understanding the trial changed too.

Trauma and denigration ceremony

In the first two months our concept was that of 'trauma'. Normally very little is publicised about the day-to-day life of schools apart from academic achievements, musical evenings and sometimes 'summer fayres'. Professor Ted Wragg, then Dean of Education at Nottingham University, had said that same year: 'there's no such thing as good news out of comprehensives. You can't get it published. The press just don't want to know.'

Yet here was 'bad news' and the reverse of that truth. There was the rancour of dispute, the polarisation of the teaching profession and public alike and cries of outrage and despair from the vast majority of staff, parents and pupils. The trauma for all the school's participants did not, however, come directly from the conflicts or even from the ever present possibility of bad news. The trauma came from the feeling of being encircled and under siege.

In another context Stuart Hall has captured an everyday aspect of the isolation of the urban school: 'the urban school visibly stranded—beached—above the retreating social landscape'.[3] Here was a secondary school beached and stranded by a blaze of publicity. In the extraordinary times through which we were studying the school it became an act of explicit commitment to go into the school or even very near it. Of course there were messages of goodwill and support but as Mike Minchin had said of similar times at Countesthorpe College: 'we had been assured that many, many people were right behind us and so they were, eight miles behind'.[4] Isolation was reinforced by heated arguments in shops and houses, sometimes with the most unexpected and thus more hurtful antagonists. Each group—staff, parents and pupils—found out who their enemies were and had their private battles with which to contend.

The community within the school became more industrious, more caring and more stoical as time went on. The great rush of initial publicity had been traumatic—in the sense of numbing, appalling and literally unthinkable. After the first months, though, a new phase began.

Quite recently Garfinkel coined the term 'denigration ceremony'[5] to describe how the medical profession tries a doctor who
is alleged to have breached the profession's ethics. The process
involves a highly publicised trial upon one or two specific charges,
and hearing 'evidence' about the character defects after revela-
tion until they have been 'pulled out' of the role of doctor
altogether. Little by little their personalities are stripped and
picked clean until they are shunned and then banished. The role
of the doctor remains intact. In keeping with the times we sought
to study the trial as a denigration ceremony.

It was soon apparent that the 'swearing incident' and all that
went with it were regarded as the head's fault and that the
denigration ceremony would be for him. As attention switched to
the man and his mannerisms there was a new kind of helplessness.
Anyone who is fully active makes mistakes; part of their skill lies
in knowing this and having others help them in making repairs.
Of course, the head had made mistakes. Sensing the build-up of a
denigration ceremony his staff put yet more energy into guessing
what mistakes of theirs might be attributed to him and putting
them right. In covering themselves and him, they actually
exposed supposed areas of weakness yet further. All manner of
protocol and procedure could reveal weaknesses or errors. Meanwhile the fact that the head seemed to be the sole target held
responsible 'for what had been going on' threatened to further
isolate him.

A semi-legal process

Yet again a concept waxed and waned. Whilst opponents did
seem determined to denigrate the head the concept of ceremony
quickly became inappropriate. This was no matter of disgrace
which would be dealt with by the profession itself. There was a
process under way in which county council politicians wanted to
hold one kind of trial and teachers' unions—and no doubt county
administrators too—wanted to hold another.

Trials are a matter of law and the new emergent concept was
that of a 'semi-legal process'. Whereas 'ceremony' implied ritual
in the sense of established routine imbued with mystical lore, here
was an incident for which English case law was being made. Such
a central aspect as this needed to be fully understood by all

participants. Once a public hearing or trial had been proposed everyone was obliged to refer to the law. Until such a moment it was quite probable that very few teachers knew the legal basis upon which their endeavours could stand or fall. Our search established that there is no mention of hearings or trials as such but rather the relevant law is concerned with inspectors and inspections. The Education Act 1944 (S.76) says:

> the Secretary of State and Local Education Authorities shall have regard to the general principle that so far as is compatible with the provision of efficient instruction and training and the avoidance of unreasonable public expenditure, pupils are to be educated in accordance with the wishes of their parents.

There is no obligation upon an authority to consult or mobilise parents' wishes generally:

> The obligation imposed by this section is to consult the wishes of the parents in regard to their own children, not to consult parents generally.[6]

But there is the matter of 'efficient instruction' which can, and should, be inspected. With regard to inspections themselves, Section 77 of the Education Act 1944 includes the following:

> It shall be the duty of the Secretary of State to cause inspections of every educational establishment at such intervals as appear to him to be appropriate and to cause a special inspection . . . to be made whenever he considers such an inspection to be desirable; and for the purpose of enabling such inspections . . . inspectors may be appointed by [Her] Majesty on the recommendation of the Secretary of State [Paragraph 2].

> Any local education authority may cause an inspection to be made by officers appointed by the Local Education Authority [Paragraph 3].

> If any person obstructs . . . the provisions of this section he shall be liable on summary conviction to a fine not exceeding twenty pounds, or in the case of a second or subsequent conviction, to a fine not exceeding fifty pounds or to imprisonment for a term not exceeding three months or to both such imprisonment and such fine [Paragraph 4].

The Act makes it necessary for the Secretary of State to have inspectors, known as Her Majesty's Inspectors, permanently on active duty and in a state of readiness for special operations. This

would seem to give HMIs two clear roles: as advisers to the local
education authority (LEA) and the Department of Education and
Science (DES); and as inspectors, which in practice is to act as
'trouble-shooters'. During the course of part of their everyday
work, HMIs may be attending to matters of 'efficient instruction'
and 'due economy'. But during the extraordinary circumstances
of conducting inspections, with which this book is concerned,
they may be involved with reconciling 'standards' with the
'wishes of the parents' and others. The same might be said of the
local authority's own inspectors.[7]

Virginia Makins's account of Countesthorpe's inspection
forges inseparable links between parents, politics and inspections:

> The worries eventually found expression in a petition by 411
> people—not all of them parents—demanding that their children
> should be given suitable and efficient education under the 1944
> Act.

> the . . . petition was welcome fuel for opponents of the school
> whose concerns were not just educational but also tied up with
> local politics.

> The publicity . . . finally led the Chairman of the Education
> Committee to ask Mrs Thatcher [then Secretary of State for
> Education] for a full inspection.[8]

A similar chain of events was occurring at Sutton Centre. It
was announced that there would be two enquiries. The local
authority would set up a 'court' of its own and there would be a
full HMI inspection in February 1978.

Trial, enquiry and inspection

It was not until the midpoint of a packed period that the
distinction between three previously interchangeable terms
became apparent. The term 'trial' was the popular or everyday
notion which brought together the face-to-face exchanges, the
media coverage, the inspection, the hearing, and linked them
finally with the question of whether the school was guilty or
innocent. The term 'trial' bridged three overlapping periods of
trial by media, trial by ordeal and trial by inspection. The very
vividness of the word 'trial' nevertheless missed aspects which the

more precise terms 'enquiry' and 'inspection' did not. For what was proposed showed that the inspectors' trouble-shooter role was beset with major ironies. First, the guidelines upon which the inspectors were to operate were not known to the subjects of the inspection and there was no mandatory obligation to reveal the results. Secondly, the visit would distort the situation being investigated. Thirdly, the timing of the inspectors' visit was linked to the more general changes in which the school was caught; and fourthly, there would be no obligation to implement the inspectors' findings. Virginia Makins neatly highlighted some of these dilemmas in respect of Countesthorpe:

> A heavy veil of secrecy, pinned down by Crown Copyright, is drawn over the workings of full inspections, and their results. (The school and the governors asked that the report should be published, but the Department of Education and Science refused.) The staff seem to have found the long discussions with individual subject inspectors extremely helpful and often supportive, but the whole occasion somewhat bizarre. The careful rituals of an inspection, no doubt evolved in the interests of maximum discretion, sat uncomfortably in a school where everything was deliberately made open to staff and students. And specific things, like the timetable analysis the inspectors use, could not be made to fit the individual timetable.[9]

An inspection is a formal event with problems of its own: the term specifically applies to the visit by HM Inspectorate or local authority inspectors and the contradictions of their role in the enquiry process. To speak of an enquiry refers to the decision to cause a visit and the reception designed to deal with its results. The visit at Sutton Centre was to be 'professional' whilst the enquiry was clearly more 'political': the enquiry included decisions already being made which were to change the fortunes of the school.

Great attention was paid towards the visit by the inspectorate. Once their formal visit was announced the matter was apparently *sub judice*. There was a set moment of silence during which the protagonists were separated. The pivot of the enquiry was said to be the formal visitation. The announcement that an inspection would take place was intended to allay fears and calm anxieties. But at the same time the authority was giving notice that changes would inevitably have to be made.

Although the full inspection was intended to be part of an
advisory function, i.e. to 'afford assistance' and not 'restrain local
efforts', it was accepted that the visit would produce emotional
stress. Indeed the formal visit was, in part, a conflict producer:
having suspended debate the parties had to repeat their arguments
against each other once again. In so doing the parties retrenched
further.

Her Majesty's Inspectors, as the most prestigious peace-
keeping force in the educational sphere, were considered to be
sufficiently expert to judge which aspects were important and
which unimportant. They represented the ultimate competence
for testing the school's strengths and weaknesses and in
advocating remedies. Yet, as has been suggested, the inspectorate
managed the moment rather than determined the future; they
'policed the crisis'.[10] The inspectors, having kept abreast of
changes within the authority and within state legislation, cast
their report accordingly. To help this work they were well
informed—so well informed as to be able to anticipate decisions
and reinforce them. The enquiry was not a proper trial in the
sense of observing courtroom procedure because there was an
Alice in Wonderland factor: it included the prospect of 'sentence
first—judgement later'.

The enquiry was also but a semi-legal process because whilst
provision was made for instituting an enquiry, there did not
appear to be any ground rules as to how it should take place. Nor
were there any legal safeguards for those being investigated. Thus
it became a 'hearing' without charges, without legal representation of the interested parties and, most particularly, without the
right of cross-examination.

The participants, meanwhile, were still largely preoccupied
with the sequence of events which had prompted the call for
investigation. The inspection became the authority's answer to
such a call whilst at the same time consideration was being given
to what 'changes would have to be made'. Therefore the inspection was not a ritual without result, it was not a harmless moment
of mumbo jumbo. Rather it was that part of the enquiry when
problems and failings were looked for entirely within the school as
if fully separated from the political process in which it was caught.

These, then, were our starting points in the months when we
realised that an inspection had been and gone, the enquiry was a
spent force and the trial was over. First we had the horrible shock

of public disgrace and the role of the media in education. Closely linked with that was the character assassination of the head. Lastly there was the sight of a legal-looking invention which had bubbled, cracked and spewed forth like a volcano beneath the feet of the participants.

Yet at this point we thought that writing up what we could about Sutton Centre would have the effect of keeping its troubles going. There were also some important connections to be made with those who had sent messages of support. After all, 'out there', there were others who had been through the same experiences. Having been on the edge of a real nightmare for so long we just had to find out what had happened to others. Our identification with the school varied considerably but we were united in believing that we had observed something far more disturbing than the daily life of Sutton Centre.

Trials and enquiries elsewhere

Even whilst the Sutton Centre struggle was taking shape, four teachers from William Tyndale Primary School, London, including the headmaster, were making some telling points as they told their side of the 'William Tyndale affair'; 'The decision to inspect the school before the enquiry was a political one'; Political decisions were to overrule the inspectors'; 'The enquiry was just another pressure without guarantees'; 'The inspection was being undertaken before anybody knew that the enquiry was going to consider and how it was going to consider it'; and the most telling rhetorical question of all: 'In the context of the enquiry, as it finally emerged, one wonders what the use of the inspection was'.[11]

William Tyndale School's enquiry was, like Sutton Centre's, also a mixture of steady motion and hasty invention. It attracted more attention in the press than any other event in postwar educational history, not least because the court enquiry itself was the most complete assembly of 'due legal process' to date and because English primary education has rarely been so riddled with conflict. We separated the process from the polemics in the ex-Tyndale staff's book and discovered many more points which could find their mark in an analysis of Sutton Centre's experience (see Appendix). We also sought out other trials and enquiries in the period since the Second World War.

After reading and discussing the available accounts it did seem that enquiries have highly selective, sinister and bizarre qualities; the professional act of 'inspection' invariably bobbed along on a tide of political process. Four comprehensive school enquiries—Risinghill Comprehensive, Islington; Summerhill Academy, Aberdeen; Countesthorpe College, Leicestershire; and Sutton Centre itself—revealed astonishing similarities as well as their own special twists and turns. By and large the earlier stories had been told in strident terms; their respective writers could be said to have been struggling for retrospective justice.

We had considerable problems with these histories. They were written by partisans and there was little other evidence available. We sought a cooler reconstruction of events in order to be able to go directly to similarities. Furthermore we had been developing a dual focus which came in the form of a double question: did the similarities lie in what the schools were trying to do, or in what happened to them? We were struck by the fact that here were four newly opened comprehensive schools which having been launched upon high hopes were then quite quickly driven aground by their owners. Once we had re-pieced the stories together it was what the schools stood for which seemed, almost incredibly, at least as important as the rigours of their trials. We came within the heartland of educational studies; we had to establish what is meant by 'innovation', 'progressive' and 'comprehensive' because in casually using these terms we found the four schools to be identical despite their differences in period.

'Innovation', 'progressive' and 'comprehensive'

John Watts succinctly put innovation into context when, writing as an educationalist, he opened a paper with: 'May I suggest that "change" is something that happens to us and that "innovation" is something that we choose to bring about.'[12]

Thus, here, innovation could mean what teachers in schools set about doing themselves and could refer to initiatives for extending their involvement and reciprocity with pupils, parents and the community at large. Innovation is in part a response to new demands – that is, to changes in political and economic life. Furthermore a school is not a closed world. As John Watts continued; this definition does not imply a conflict-free laboratory for good intentions. There is considerable debate over what changes innovation is in response to and what changes it brings about. There is also dispute over whether innovation is a 'good thing'. As John Watts wrote: 'one man's innovation is another man's change'.[13] Or as Barry MacDonald recast this axiom in terms of struggles within the teaching profession: 'It is naive to think of educational change as a game which everyone wins, seductive though that is. One man's bandwagon is another man's hearse.'[14] The important point is, we feel, that innovation is continuous change. John Watts:

> We must innovate or crumble and we must innovate not so as to produce a permanent new solution but in the hopes of creating mutable systems, themselves open to continuous modification, ever sensitive to new needs.[15]

It remains an open question what internally generated and sustained change actually applies to. John Watts related two innovatory sequences: the working agreement made between teacher and student (where choice and negotiation lead to a 'contract') and 'individualized programmes of study in school, resource-based learning and consequent community involvement'. Thus innovation refers to more than tinkering with technique, it means a movement of greater complexity and interrelatedness. In all our four case studies there were innovations in roles, relationships and the relative values given to the school subjects studied. More significantly perhaps there was a culture and climate of innovation which were especially concerned with making the school more 'open'.

It was not difficult to see why innovation and 'progressive' were so often hitched together in the same harness. 'Progressivism' is a much older educational concept: it refers to creating and sustaining the autonomy of the learner. Progressivism can be traced back to Pestalozzi and probably yet further still. Unlike innovation it refers to a fundamental position in education in which supreme value is given to the learner and learning. In contemporary times progressivism has often found a political expression, particularly in response to the questions, Who does learning belong to?, How should learning be organised?

and What is the place of school in society? As we were engaged on these matters Roger Dale produced the first analysis of the 'levels' of dispute manifested by the William Tyndale staff:

> The teachers ignored or denied the functions they were—implicity of course—expected to perform . . . Their job was not to provide 'factory fodder'; they saw themselves as preparing human beings rather than human capital.
>
> This approach was complemented at a political level by the encouragement of questioning rather than blind obedience among the pupils, and by the denial of hierarchical relationships both within the staff and between the staff and pupils.
>
> . . . at the ideological level came . . . the techers' vehement denial of the 'neutrality' of schooling and their explicitly socialist philosophy.[16]

The significance of 'progressive' for us was that some teachers and some commentators referred to our case study schools as progressive: because they were responding to the first 'level', to 'preparing human beings rather than human capital'. It was apparent to us, too, that whilst 'denial of hierarchy' was an overstatement of their aims and achievements, there were democratic forms emerging or established in the schools. Finally whatever the value positions of their teaching staff themselves, comprehensives had derived from an 'explicitly socialist philosophy'.

Reynolds and Sullivan define the British comprehensive experience as: 'the movement towards and the effects of the introduction of unified schooling for children of all abilities'.[17] The proposal to adopt comprehensive schooling was official Labour Party policy at the 1964 election. Reynolds and Sullivan suggest that the policy had three linked goals: a greater development of talent, the reduction and in the longer term the removal of inequalities of opportunity and the reduction of adolescent deviance. They continue:

> A substantial number of liberal educational reforms followed, then, in the mid and late 1960s. Expenditure on education was almost doubled as a proportion of the Gross National Product. The school leaving age was to be raised to 16 . . . A veritable plethora of innovations in the field of curriculum design and curriculum evaluation were also launched together with . . . the Circular 10/65 which was issued requesting local authorities to submit plans

for the reorganization of their schools upon comprehensive and non selective lines.[18]

Comprehensives would be opposed by those who subscribed to the grammar school/secondary modern school model. This opposition was actually helped by the lack of further guidance from the Labour Party, the DES and HMI. Whatever was to become of comprehensives was therefore more likely to depend upon what local politicians, parents and the teaching profession could come to mutual terms upon. Despite great expectations amongst some professionals, the result was often a large non-selective grammar school with tiers of hierarchy and some curriculum development for pupils who were hard to teach.

There were social class undercurrents beneath this drift back to grammar schools. The middle-class values of academic attainment and character moulding were pursued by ex-grammar school head teachers at the helm of schools twice the size or more of those with which they had previously had experience. Another middle-class value, 'good management', was a salve for their struggles with size, whilst a 'charitable concern' for lower stream pupils helped with the problems of 'keeping them on at school'.

Thus there was flat political opposition to dismantling centres of decorum and privilege; there was hardly any leadership from those who usually gave it and there was the re-emergence of the grammar school whereby middle-class parents, the sixth form subscribers, could be mollified into believing that standards had after all been maintained.

We found a veritable mountain of rhetoric about comprehensives, what they were, could be or should be. We also found that most sociologists thought there was no good news from comprehensives either. The very question, What is a comprehensive? was becoming unanswerable as there was so little middle ground between these two positions: either comprehensives were the first indistinct rays of a new dawn in which precise forms could not yet be distinguished; or they were direct reproductions of the existing structure of social relations. Yet between these two extremes were our case studies: determined efforts to realise a comprehensive form, content and broad purposes. They had had a flying start by being new comprehensives perhaps. Or perhaps their heads and staff were most untypical. The point was that they had openly struggled towards what they called comprehensive ideals and innovated in sequences which could be described as progressive processes.

Then David Hargreaves's book *The Challenge of the Comprehensive School*[19] was published. This was Hargreaves's first major writing to be intended for teachers and administrators. We had come to the same position, although without such concreteness and clarity. Hargreaves wrote: 'I am convinced that there should be more dialogue between academics and teachers . . . this book is directed to the audience of practising teachers rather than to my academic colleagues.'[20]

Hargreaves clarified the essential question of who we were writing for and why we were writing for them. We, too, were concerned to communicate directly with intending and practising teachers. Our brief excursion into the descriptive categories of innovation, progressivism and comprehensive had the consequence of telling us how our case studies could be broadly described but had not fully come to grips, as Hargreaves had, with the emerging, altering nature of their efforts.

This gave our critical incidents something more than the significance of cautionary tales. It was crucial to us that these histories be seen both as accounts of what comprehensive schools could be and as trials which need not occur in such forms again. We resolved to take up the issue of the near defencelessness of these schools. It was this defencelessness which had been the major obstacle to their development. By implication the same defencelessness could be felt by all comprehensive schools in which innovation and progressivism were live issues.

Contemporary concerns

Two recent political decisions reinforced our resolution. The two decisions were to replace 'catchment areas' for schools with 'parental choice' and to publish HMI reports. 'Catchment areas' for comprehensives had been based, in turn, upon 'feeder primary schools'. A comprehensive school's size averaged 1,500 pupils and could be as large as 2,000 pupils or more. This size had its institutional strengths as well as the organisational problems mentioned previously. With the general allowance (the per capita grant) resources could be bought and maintained quite comprehensive—scientific equipment, books, video and reprographic machinery. With the staffing provision (the total scale points available to the head) a comprehensive curriculum could be developed; in theory it would be possible to teach a range of subjects that was almost as broad as the credentialling procedures of 'O' level and CSE would allow.

The two concurrent strengths of comprehensives depended upon the 'pupils on roll'. Thus when a feed of pupils from neighbouring (and distant) primaries was no longer guaranteed the general allowance and staffing provision became much less predictable. The plain fact was that aspiring and middle-class parents could send their children to one of a number of schools, once again putting a projected sixth form into a highly competitive vice. The unease which this caused would inevitably become anxiety when the 'falling rolls' of primary schools became the diminishing pupil numbers in comprehensives. A downward spiral was predictable: a reduction in resources and staffing making the school less competitive and so on. Schools, like those in our case studies, which did not compete on the same terms as those in the mainstream would be exposed to the risk of local children being sent elsewhere. When mounting parental concern over the likelihood of youth unemployment clutched at the straw of examination successes as the critical *raison d'être* of secondary education, a profile of innovation and progressivism could look a distinctly threatening future prospect for their children. In brief, teachers could have the stuffing knocked out of their will and wish to innovate. All this made it yet more important to put on record what our case study schools had been doing.

The second decision in the early 1980s could have some significance for the trials of 'high profile' innovatory schools. All regular HMI inspections, held at five- to seven-year intervals it was said, would be published in full. This decision was heralded as a 'watershed' for public accountability. Yet on the basis of our case studies we could not see how the publication of reports could aid schools which were underoing the extraordinary circumstances of trials. HMI reports might feed persuasion and support into the ordinary life of schools, but our studies had shown that HMI were more likely to be either excluded from or incorporated within schools on trial. We also needed to recall the trial processes, therefore, to show how this might be so.

Madeley Court's trial

As if to prove the point, Madeley Court School went on trial in 1983. Shropshire County Council published two reports later that year. The first was the work of four county councillors—the chairman of the council assisted by the chairman of the education committee and two other members. They tried to sort out what went wrong. The second group made suggestions for what they thought would be 'improvements' at the school.

The first report does indeed plot a history. It traces tensions from the day the school opened through to the second head's appointment and then features the chief education officer, his advisers, the head, his governors and staff. Only at the end do HMI appear. The following excerpts make this clear:[21]

> Para.3.2.1. The school's first Headmaster, Mr Hugh Cunningham (1971–1977), faced a number of problems. [These included] an innovative design calling for a radical approach to organisation and method of teaching . . . and the divided management responsibilities for the school and Joint Use Centre.

> 3.2.2. Of the six candidates selected for interview, four withdrew. The appointing body spent some considerable time discussing whether to go ahead with the appointment but decided to do so. Mr Toogood had impressed the body on interview . . . he had some seven years' experience as Head of a village college in Cambridgeshire . . . At the appointment it was made clear to Mr Toogood that the LEA did not intend to develop Madeley Court as a community school *in the sense of the Head being responsible for the provision of further education and organising recreational activities for the community.* Mr Toogood accepted this.

> 3.2.5. One predominating matter which occupied the Headmaster and Governors' attention . . . was the Head's wish, contrary to LEA policy. to develop community education and *his dislike of the divided managerial responsibilities for the school and the Joint Use Centre.*

> 3.2.6. The CEO made it plain to the head that his proposals for using the school and its staff for community purposes were out of line with the County Council's policy. It is plain, equally, that despite this the Head continued, *with the support of his Governors,* to pursue this theme, and at one stage designated one of his staff as Head of Community Education.

3.2.8. The school was visited by advisers from time to time . . . *none saw the school as presenting particular problems requiring special attention*. It is worthy of note that in this period the advisers were heavily committed elsewhere in the county.

3.3.1. *From the evidence that was given to us* the first that the Education Department perceived of anything wrong in the school was in the early summer of 1980 when *it came to the Department's notice* that a number of staff *were said to have resigned* with no other job to go to and that the morale of the staff was low . . . This was reinforced by a letter addressed to the governors and signed by ten senior members of the staff.

3.3.2. This matter was considered in depth at a special governors' meeting attended by the Assistant County Education Officer and the then Chief Adviser from which *it was plain that the Governors supported the Headmaster*. As a result of this meeting it was agreed that the two county officers should join the senior management of the school to help them review its organisation and curriculum.

3.3.3. In choosing this form of review the Chief Adviser had very much in mind the fact that the school had *an unusually high degree of staff involvement in the processes of curriculum development and forward planning*. This had been very much Mr Toogood's wish . . . It was clear to us that the Governors regarded the Curriculum Review as the professionals' intervention . . . and they had an almost unquestioning confidence in the success of this intervention.

3.3.6. In the months following the Curriculum Review the CEO came to the view that he needed a comprehensive and objective assessment of the school. He also recognised that he would have little prospect of influencing the Head, *or if necessary taking disciplinary action against him*, unless he had an authoritative assessment which would bear independent examination. *This latter point being particularly important where . . . the Head appeared to have the full support of his Governors*.

3.3.9. The CEO discussed the possibility of the Authority's Advisory staff carrying out inspection of the school but decided that there was no possibility of this since the Chief Adviser had just retired and there were five vacancies in the team.

3.3.8. Accordingly the CEO decided that the only course open to him was to invite HMI to carry out a formal inspection.

3.3.10. In the year 1981—82 although the Advisory Team continued to visit they . . . *plainly did not consider that the school merited unusual attention, and the then Chief Adviser told us that despite his criticisms he did not consider the school to be 'in a disaster situation'.*

3.3.12. Twice during the autumn of 1981 the CEO visited the school and a summary of available advisers' views given to him before his second visit, covering Maths, Science, Music and Art, *was not unfavourable. His own visit led him to be more critical of the Headmaster* . . . But he was conscious that *without a full and detailed investigation his criticisms would be superficial.*

3.3.13. In January 1982 a new governing body took office. *Only one of the previous members remaining.*

3.3.15. The HMI Inspection took place. At the end of March the Report was published.

3.3.16. The Head felt unable to comply with the requirements *specified by the county education officer at the request of the (new) Governors.* The Head tendered his resignation which was accepted.

Here, then, were the bare bones of a power struggle and some of the factors, e.g. the departure of the supporting governors, which tipped the swaying balance. There was but one mention of innovation and none of parents or even pupils. Moves were made and tracks were laid which would quite probably affect their lives. But the report made this trial seem a matter of public accountability behind closed doors.

It was obvious that we had come full circle, that we should reconstruct the trials as dramatic events and follow these accounts with a framework for their understanding. Only in that way could we make the relationships between actors and action as apparent as it now seemed. We were spurred on by advance publicity for Phillip Toogood's own book, *A Head's Tale*, about which he says in relation to his own carreer that one aim is:

> To try to unravel the tangled experience of those of us who set out in the 60s to build an authentic comprehensive, community based system of education . . . I situate the crisis at Madeley Court within this journey and trace the roots of the problem to the grim evidence, now more apparent than ever, that our strivings to build a common school system since 1867 have been overborne by social policy designed to perpetuate a stratified and divided society. Uppingham, though I was very happy there, epitomised this. Wyndham was a transitional comprehensive, caught by the deep

dichotomy between 'school' and 'college' sides which the incoming commuter population at the end of the new M11 strove hard to perpetuate. Only at Madeley Court did we begin to engage in that approach to integration with community by the device of the 'mini-school' which seemed able to contrive both that sense of belonging and adventure in learning that leads to an integrated experience. Here, however, by the accident of policies designed to reinforce reaction, the chasm of benign indifference to community education eventually led to our efforts being swallowed up.

What Toogood seemed to be saying related back to Roger Dale's second level: community education as expressed in the 'device' of a 'mini-school' was an alternative to hierarchy and hierarchical control. In that respect his philosophy was but one more contemporary version of philosophies first held at Risinghill School, Summerhill Academy, Countesthorpe College and Sutton Centre. What brought the case studies together was their concern for democracy – in learning, in daily school life and in preparation for later life. A comparison of their aims and developments could bring this once again into the foreground.

In contrast were their trials. The obstacles to the emergence of democratic comprehensives appeared to be subterranean and systematically placed. The issues for this book became two questions and a search for a particular answer to them: what do the trials of democratic comprehensives tell us about those schools and about 'politics with a small p'? And how can the latter's essentially undemocratic nature be overcome?

The shape of the book

There are aspects of this book with which we are still not satisfied. We open with three cases taken from secondary sources. These are arranged in chronological order. The further back in recent history they are the fewer the sources. The first two, in fact, are more like the story of the schools' heads than the schools' lives. Also, they are drawn from such strong polemics that their 'other sides' are too faintly given. Even when we checked our accounts we did so only with the two respective heads. They are more subjective and skeletal than we would have liked.

Countesthorpe College's account is larger and fuller because there were more sources and participants who could criticise our drafts. It also brings out more sub-themes and offers insights into the heads' potential roles in 'politics with a small p'. Sutton Centre's trial is where we began and yet more fully written—partly as a result of our investigations and partly because it has not, to our knowledge, appeared elsewhere in print before.

We have already indicated the setting for our conclusion, namely the steps to be taken for democratic comprehensives to sustain and be sustained. We can draw lessons of some significance from a clutch of case studies, and we have attempted to do so in Chapter 9. We can also argue for changes in practice—both within schools and within their trials—and Chapter 10 does so as a result of what we have learned.

Having told our story it is time to retell that of those who went on trial.

Part one

Comprehensive school trials from 1959 to 1974

1

'Barbed wire beyond the cage':
Risinghill's reforms rejected

we will send out children who are not well mannered, not interested in a wide range of subjects, and not competent in basic skills . . . It might be legitimate in an independent school to adopt his methods, but they could not be tolerated in a state school.[1]

Michael Duane's earlier career

Ex-major Duane left the army in 1946 with an exemplary reference from his Brigadier. In 1948, at the age of thirty-three, he became the first head of Howe Dell, a secondary modern school near Hatfield. The director of education, John Newsom, gave him 'five years with no questions asked'[2] to set the new school on its feet. Until Howe Dell was ready Michael Duane was head of Beaumont Secondary Modern School in St Albans for one term. In an end-of-term message John Newsom wrote:

If you can do what you have done at Beaumont's then there is no doubt that the Old Rectory at Hatfield will soon become one of the greatest jewels in our educational crown! We are all most indebted to you and encouraged for the future.[3]

A visiting academic summed up Howe Dell in the following terms:

(a) There was the head's commitment to the children and to parent—child relationships.
(b) Emotional needs were considered as important as academic standards.
(c) The staff explained their aims to parents in their homes.
(d) The prime aim was self-discipline.
(e) There was no corporal punishment.
(f) Informal relationships between staff and children were encouraged.[4]

Duane was also openly committed to multi-racial education. An Alderman Maynard protested that a 'sex film, with a black man and white woman' had been shown at Howe Dell. In fact, the film was a Cyril Bibby film-strip in human physiology[5] depicting male figures shaded more strongly than the female. All the same the county council appointed an enquiry committee whose members included Alderman Maynard. The enquiry found that there was 'no evidence of indecent interest' but they were disturbed at Duane's apparent lack of concern. The enquiry committee, having warmed to its task, moved onto discuss other related matters. They decided that 'the time, the place and the opportunity for undesirable horse-play ought not to be given'. They ordered that a barn where the children played should be put out of bounds and their outdoor playing space curtailed.

Michael Duane was appointed a Justice of the Peace and subsequently in April sat on the same bench as Alderman Maynard who was chairman of magistrates. Moving yet closer on a collision course, Duane was nominated as Labour candidate for a seat that had been held for a long time by a Conservative who was also the husband of one of his governors. John Newsom wrote to Duane asking if it was discreet to take on public duties when his school was not yet well established and warning him that he had had to listen to a lot of comment on this subject lately. Duane tried to cancel his candidature but was too late. Alderman Maynard, as chairman of the county council staffing sub-committee, passed on to Duane a committee decision forbidding him to sit on the bench during school hours.

Within two years the school received a special enquiry, a special visit by an HMI, a check by two of the authority's inspectors and finally a full inspection. Each denounced the policy which Duane had set out to implement. After the full HMI inspection, Mr Maynard, as chairman of the governors, stated 'there must be no risk of variations from the traditional'[6] and insisted that the headmaster use the cane in school. Michael Duane considered taking legal action but Mr Newsom advised him to resign. He moved to a headship in Lowestoft.

Two years later the Lowestoft school also had an inspection and was given a good report. John Newsom congratulated Duane on this achievement.

Risinghill

In 1959, despite his previous conflicts and his teachers' union and Labour Party activities, Michael Duane returned to London and his fourth headship. The school was Risinghill in Islington. 'Islington is not, on the whole, a district of delight';[7] Risinghill was set in a troubled and potentially hostile environment.

In 1960 four secondary schools (a mixed secondary school, a girls' secondary school, a boys' technical secondary school and a girls' technical school), plus eleven-year-olds from a local primary school, were all amalgamated to form Risinghill. The children who came directly from the local primary school already had a history of being uprooted through previous school closures. About one quarter of the children were not English, and came from nineteen different nationalities in all. A section of the community were being helped by care committees, the National Society for Prevention of Cruelty to Children and other welfare agencies. The neighbourhood grammar schools drew intelligent children of ambitious parents away, with the result that Risinghill did not have its declared quota of high ability range pupils. Ninety of the intake were on probation for various offences, mainly 'breaking and entering'.

The amalgamation of the four schools into Risinghill was unpopular with many of their staffs and half of Risinghill's staff came from the previous four schools. Two ex-heads, in particular, were obliged to adopt a philosophy with which they had little sympathy. The staff room divided itself into men at one end and women at the other. The staff were used to direct leadership from the head; Michael Duane said: 'All our problems of discipline and organisation stemmed from this. They did not know how to deal with children who are uninhibited and therefore a threat to authoritarian standards . . . and they were not trained for a big school where the Head is not present as a perpetual father figure and continually within reach to sort everything out for them.'[8]

The school buildings were a problem, too, with six separate playgrounds and scattered drab buildings on a sloping waterlogged site, no covered play space, and no soundproofing. The large amount of unstrengthened glass made the place like an oven in summer and an icebox in winter; lack of safety catches on the sliding windows meant that a child could fall out—as sadly one did. The administrative side of the education service had flatly advised against putting a new school at Risinghill Street. When the same administrators saw the plans of the building they said it was unworkable.

A greater problem—greater than a staff amalgamated by shot-gun, buildings which were unsuitable and children of many different races—was, in Duane's opinion, whether or not the comprehensive school was regarded as a promise or a threat by the majority of the parents. In his view:

> The politicians never considered the possibility that to working class people in a country that is just beginning to move socially from feudalism, for whom social value and position has hitherto appeared to be ordained by God, a neighbourhood comprehensive school can look like a threat; that is, can seem to be a cunning scheme to hold them back, a new way of trapping those who at last see a chance of getting out, the barbed wire beyond the cage.[9]

Right from the start the new school was saddled with both practical and psychological stresses.

Early differences, difficulties and developments

The responsibility for caning lay with the head and Michael Duane was wholly opposed to corporal punishment which he believed was 'both brutal and encouraged brutality'. He was at odds with the actual practice of the London County Council (LCC) which, in 1959, had issued a confidential booklet advising teachers how children should be hit with either of the two approved canes, and on what part of the body. Instead he agreed with the pamphlet recommending the progressive abandonment of corporal punishment, a pamphlet also issued to every new head in 1959.

Duane refused to expel anyone. He said that since education had been made compulsory by the state, expulsion was illegal. So he took children other heads had expelled, and did everything in his power to keep them from being sent away from their homes to approved schools or Borstals. The absence of corporal punishment and the preparedness to provide a refuge placed a great reliance on the strength of informal relationships.

None of the authority's inspectors with a brief to report on Risinghill agreed with the abolition of corporal punishment and they complained that Duane had a lax attitude towards discipline. On the other hand the HMI, Fred Munday, whilst doubtful about full abolition, a year later told Duane in the presence of another HMI that the decision had been right.

The two ex-heads on the staff believed that children were being ruined at Risinghill; that they were becoming impudent and undisciplined and were also reverting to home accents. Some of the 'home accents' referred to were entire languages. Duane took on Greek, Turkish, African and West Indian teachers to cater for the needs of the immigrant pupils. School letters to parents were sent in their own languages, so that they could understand what was being done. 'If "comprehensive education" means anything,' said Michael Duane, 'it must mean that everyone has riches to contribute to the common treasure. How can any school that assumes the all-importance of Englishness ever do this?'[10] The school began to be known as a place where people of all nationalities could come for advice. The educational attaché and the welfare officer from the Greek Embassy came to see the school.

Two kinds of difficulty were met by direct provision. First, pupils with major learning problems could meet in small groups with one teacher in a 'specialist' room. Secondly, the school's heads of house had 'family' duties as well as teaching duties in an effort to cope with pupils' problems of anonymity. Duane reasoned that what was needed was 'special teachers within the school taking groups of children who needed therapeutic treatment and nursing them back to the normal teaching situation'.

Risinghill's school council became the focus for discussing all disputes and complaints. It was made up of four teachers (including the head himself), twelve pupils and three other adults working in the school. Anyone with a grievance could ask for a meeting of the school council, a situation which exacerbated the fraught relationships in the staff room as teachers felt that they were being criticised. This arrangement led to the LCC inspector being informed by dissident teachers that teacher authority was being undermined by this 'democratic ploy'.

Michael Duane, for his part, thought not so much about teachers' rights as about human rights. He asked the LCC to look at the broad social situation of children who arrived very early at school and then caused vandalism. He wanted these children to be allowed within school early so that they could have extra tuition, or do homework, or read or talk. But some teachers said this provision was 'disorganised' and 'chaotic' and debarred their children from early entry. Other teachers, though, did come early and stay late to help the children. It was difficult to arrange such after-school events, even though several teachers tried to. LCC inspector McGowan, however, said that the social problems of the children were not the teachers' concern. Parents were encouraged to come to school at any time unheralded, and some teachers again resented the 'intrusion'.

A part of the multi-racial policy were Humanist assemblies. The 1962 Christmas nativity involved all nationalities. The chairman of the governors said of the occasion, 'I myself think that it is a very large part of education. The difficulty is you can't measure it.' However, the London authority, faced simultaneously with schools filled with immigrant children and a great shortage of teachers, maintained that immigrant children should be 'integrated'. In 1963, the LCC's new director of education, Dr Briault, wrote to Michael Duane:

> While sympathising with the desire to foster knowledge of the language and culture of the place of birth of immigrant minorities I do not feel this can in any sense be regarded as the responsibility of London schools. The task of the schools is really the reverse.[11]

In contrast stood part of Duane's speech-day address:

> Love thy neighbour . . . You cannot educate against the climate of opinion or attitude in the family, the neighbourhood or society. If our society were to give up the hypocritical pretence that this is a Christian country activated by Christian principles when the difference between the wealthy and the poor is so blatant, and

were to bend its efforts to making Christian love or basic democracy a reality, then there would be no limit to the progress we
could achieve with our children.[12]

   Teachers and pupils were setting down and many visitors from
abroad visited the school. One foreign teacher (acknowledging
the extreme social deprivations of the district) wrote to the British
Council, 'I strongly recommend you to include this school on
your list of interesting educational experiments for the benefit of
visitors to your country.'
   Duane was accepting invitations to speak to many organisations including a committee of MPs at the House of Commons,
the National Association for Mental Health, the Royal College of
Nursing and the Royal Society of Medicine. The Central Office
of Information sent a representative to Risinghill to prepare a
booklet for use in Cyprus. An optimistic spirit prevailed in the
school and enterprising plans were being made. Risinghill was
developing both a community centre and an arts centre. 'The
children of the school may not have realised it at the time but
they were specially privileged because they were part of something
bigger than only themselves, yet something in which they formed
the warm, living, important nucleus.'[13]

Trial by ordeal – 1961 – 3

The authority's own inspector, Mr McGowan, was amongst the
first to find fault with Risinghill's philosophy and practice. Mr
McGowan was interested in 'grammar school material' as well as
being committed to the use of corporal punishment. How does an
inspector oppose a head? In practice, Duane found that he had
little support for what needed to be done and considerable
opposition to what he wanted to do. Without Inspector
McGowan's support, problems associated with the site were to
remain unsolved. As far as opposition was concerned, McGowan
found he had allies on the staff for every kind of reason. Some
teachers found him very ready to accept complaints. For example,
at a school council meeting the head boy said some members of
staff were not turning up for playground duty as arranged and
prefects were therefore having to double up for them. Teachers
did not like being criticised and reported the incident to

McGowan. Since he was visiting the school two or three times a week during the first two years he was easily contacted.

When Risinghill opened, a third of the staff vacancies were still not filled, which resulted in a stream of supply teachers, many of whom had little teaching experience. The head claimed that many of the discipline and organisational problems stemmed from this. It was not only the children who initially had 'problems' in not having an authoritarian figurehead to coerce them, but it appeared that many staff wanted the head to have a stronger directive control than he was prepared to exert. His refusal to espouse caning and expulsion gave qualms to some staff members. The regular staff meetings (two per week at the outset) became more irregular as intransigent factions persistently argued their case regarding corporal punishment. Leila Berg's 1968 account holds that both 'traditional' teachers and most of the Communist members of staff ranged against the child-centred approach of Duane and his supporters. Having a sympathetic inspector able and willing to listen to them undoubtedly encouraged communication with Mr McGowan.

The staff and head were under stress from circumstances well beyond their control. In 1961 eight teachers left; seven for promotion and one for retirement. In addition, an artist who taught boys on probation received a letter from the divisional officer claiming that she had what amounted to a private studio free of charge at the school, and that she was to leave. This coupled with a cut of ten teachers meant the school lost the use of one workshop, one housecraft room, two art rooms and one science lab.

Also in 1961, a year after the school opened, the chairman of the governors, a Labour Party member who supported Duane, was removed from the LCC education committee because of an election technicality. Later in the year she was removed from the chairmanship of the Risinghill governors and there followed other changes in the structure of the governing body.

That same year Mr Duane had been confront by County Hall officials after he had given a lesson in sex education to adolescent boys and girls. He published an uncensored account for his staff, inspectors and governors. Later an anonymous version of the lesson was published in a Family Planning Association journal. He was summoned to County Hall to justify his actions. At this stormy meeting the director put the problem very plainly indeed:

'Comprehensive schools are a hot political issue, and . . . the LCC must have the right image. He didn't want to give "their enemies" any handle.'[14] Duane was guilty, in fact, of keeping comprehensives in the news when the politicians and administrators were desperately anxious to keep them out of the limelight. It was not merely what he was doing but the way he was doing it that was upsetting County Hall. His refusal to respond to such advice further antagonised his employers.

In January 1962, the University of London's Institute of Education asked Duane to allow one of Professor James's research students, a Lebanese teacher, to investigate relations between white and coloured children at Risinghill. The subsequent discussions in class, based on Duane's belief that 'open discussion in circumstances where calm enquiry can prevail reduces tension', caused hostile reactions from some teachers. Duane was accused of spreading racial hatred and the matter was taken to County Hall. The LCC told Duane the survey must stop immediately. The Communist teacher group also took the matter to the North London Teachers' Association—a branch of the National Union of Teachers—which passed a resolution deploring what was going on at Risinghill. Duane resigned membership of the NUT but was persuaded by union leaders to remain.

During the same month, January 1962, twenty LCC inspectors 'informally' visited Risinghill. The teachers who most rigidly opposed Duane had spent a lot of time with Inspector McGowan. They had prepared a long list of complaints. The inspectors' informal report deplored the situation which they found. Their criticisms concluded that the head did not use corporal punishment; there were graffiti-covered walls; truancy proliferated; the cordiality of the head failed to inculcate respect; some exemplary housemasters and mistresses carried burdensome responsibilities and felt compelled to look for jobs elsewhere; more central control and direction were essential; the school council was ineffective; there was an atmosphere of indiscipline.

As Leila Berg put it, 'the staff is always keyed up when Inspectors come. It was depressing to feel out of favour at County Hall . . . It was most damaging to morale. Comments by staff were interpreted to undermine Michael Duane. When it became known that Inspectors and the LCC were gunning for the school, the primary Heads and feeder primary schools knew they weren't supposed to send children.' It was as if the school began to be closed in 1962.

The inspectors decided: 'A greater measure of central control and direction is essential. Sometimes in avoiding terror, the school has abandoned awe.'[15] The report drew a firm line between the head and his staff, denounced one and praised the other, while carefully isolating, disapproving and warning the younger teachers. Dr Briault described it as 'the blackest report' he had ever seen. Summoned to County Hall to confront several officials, Duane was advised to get legal representation and meanwhile bring back corporal punishment and expulsion. He refused to do so. After the report some staff felt yet more free to work against Duane's policy. They now had the expressed view of inspectors to guide them. Staff subsequently boycotted the school council, which then died.

In July 1961, Mr Munday, the regular Ministry of Education inspector, had come for his annual visit and, in complete contrast, warmly applauded Michael Duane's policies. Then in the summer of 1962 three LCC inspectors returned to make a follow-up report – which was glowing in praise. The 'lack of leadership', 'lack of unity of purpose' and 'confusion' of the previous twenty inspectors were transformed into warm comments upon 'the most encouraging team-work'. Duane and the senior staff laughed at this, because they had changed very little of importance in the school and knew that the structural situation had not substantially altered. In practical terms, however, things were improving. The 'A' level examination results showed that pupils were being successful.

Nineteen sixty-three was a year in the balance for Risinghill. The job of moving school furniture about diminished as a sympathetic inspector recognised the situation and ordered hundreds of extra chairs; 1963 also saw the outcome of the Newsom Report (Mr Newsom now being chairman of the Central Advisory Council for Education). In an LCC follow-up enquiry of secondary schools related to the implementation of the Newsom Report, Risinghill had two mentions, and the whole section on the house system was a direct quote from Mr Duane. After the second report on Risinghill had been compiled, the district inspector, Inspector McGowan, left; even the 'enemy' was leaving. Rumour had it that only a few important people on the LCC, perhaps three, were against the school. In spite of these aspects in Risinghill's favour there was no turning point in the sense that the school became accepted, established or even was left alone. During 1963 the struggle for future years was gradually being lost. London's child population was declining, and while grammar schools took their full quota of the higher ability ranges, schools like Risinghill took the remainder.

A February 1964 article in *Punch*, which was sympathetic to the way disciplinary problems were tackled in a school with a multi-racial intake, refocused LCC attention on the school, and the ensuing education committee row was featured in the *Daily Mail*. Alderman Sebag-Montefiore, Tory Whip on the LCC, had drawn press and TV attention on the school through his articulate criticisms. The majority of coverage was sympathetic to the school, but the idea of closing the school was mooted. The newly appointed chief inspector warned Mr Duane there should be no more press publicity. He gave notice that a Ministry inspection, which occurred every seven years, would take place at Risinghill soon (opened four years previously).

Duane, after three full years, assessed the problems facing Risinghill. They were, in July 1964:

1. A shortage of qualified and experienced staff and a high turnover.
2. A school population with widely varying backgrounds.
3. A complex site difficult to administer and supervise.
4. An open site exposed to outside view.
5. An environment where prostitution, larceny and violence were common and even murder not unknown.
6. Many parents antagonistic to values of school.
7. A dearth of high ability children (½ or 1 per cent) and a plenitude of low ability children (nearly 50 per cent including educationally sub-normal children).

Duane's assessment concentrates on the problems of running a school. There is no reference to opposition from inspectors, administrators and politicians. Remarkably, parents are seen as more worthy of comment.

Closure as a solution to an employer's problem

At the beginning of the next academic year, Mr Munday HMI returned along with six more inspectors to spend four days in school. It was not a full inspection but 'a look at the academic side of the school'. One inspector, Leonard Clark, known to be particularly against comprehensive schools, vehemently attacked offences such as rude drawings in the margins of books, unmarked exercises and finding a bottle in a lavatory pan. Other antagonistic comments were directed at particular teachers. The report was delivered verbally and privately to County Hall by the hostile Inspector Clark. In his own introductory remarks Mr Munday had said that if a more broad-based inspection of the school were made — as against a merely academic one — a very different picture of the school would have emerged.

The HMI's report was to go to the DES (replacing the Ministry in April 1964) along with a recommendation that the school be closed. When Duane was summoned to County Hall by the chief inspector and the deputy education officer he was criticised for not creating 'a good image', and told that Risinghill would have to be 'reorganised'.

Knowing that the school was scheduled to close, little effort was made by the LCC to replace the staff members and deputy head who were leaving. A governor claimed, 'In the last twelve months . . . we have to make do with what the Divisional Office sends.' Tensions brought scenes between teachers. In addition, Mr Duane blotted his copybook yet again by writing a letter to the *Daily Telegraph* about comprehensive schools. The letter was in reply to an article by Angus Maude which praised the Conservatives on their educational record. The LCC saw Duane's reply as an infringement of the council's standing orders. Correspondence which had direct political implications had to be submitted to the council's press officer first, though this rule had not been invoked for similar letters written by other more amenable heads of comprehensive schools.

Three weeks later Duane was called to County Hall to be told that Risinghill was to be closed. He was accused of making slanderous statements about various people concerned with Risinghill, including members of the LCC, and of making irresponsible remarks about corporal punishment in a published article. Duane offered his resignation to the chairman of the governors but it was not accepted. The LCC claimed Risinghill was being closed because of reorganisation; Kingsway College of Further Education's need for more accommodation was urgent, although the principal, Mr Fred Flower, when asked by the press, was unaware of any unusual urgency. The necessary reorganisation meant phasing out Risinghill. The governing body reluctantly accepted the necessity of closing the school.

Reactions but no reprieve

In early January 1965 the closure of the school became public news. On 10 January, the *Sunday Times* featured Risinghill on its front page, its page-three headline read: 'LCC is Closing Toughest School'. Other national newspapers took their cue over the next few days. The *Sun* and the *Guardian* quoted a local Labour councillor who referred to teachers being beaten up and schoolgirls becoming pregnant. The *Mail* featured a seven-inch depth headline: 'The High Price of Being Ahead of Your Time'. The *Telegraph* ran the headline: 'Insults to our Head—Protest by Prefects'. The Cyprus High Commission's cultural attaché asked, 'How can you close a school which has achieved what even the United Nations has not managed to do?'[16]

In the school a different attitude existed after the announcement. Twelve children did not turn up for their GCE examinations. Children were saying that some staff had stopped bothering because they had their new schools to think about. At Easter, the equivalent of a whole would-be sixth form left. Rumours billowed about smashing up the school.

Antagonistic staff yet more openly expressed their discontent with Duane. 'If you don't like the captain, you change your ship, you don't sink the ship and everyone else on it,' he replied. 'In this school, we have had good teachers, some of the best I have ever met in my life. And we have had bad ones, the worst I have ever met, who have brought us a lot of trouble.'

Again, as in his earlier controversies, a strong reaction in favour of the school quickly surfaced. The sixth form sent a deputation to County Hall requesting the reorganisation plan to be reconsidered, bearing in mind that some of them had 'O' and

'A' level examinations to take, but this carried no weight. Other pupils back from seeing the DES commented: 'People don't understand about this school. You can't understand if you don't know Mr Duane.' An emergency meeting of 160–200 parents at the school examined the implications of the closure and culminated in a motion of confidence in the school being despatched to the LCC, the Prime Minister and the Secretary of State for Education. A deputation was elected to represent parental support of the school and its headmaster to the LCC.

These angry parents did meet the LCC. Five or six other parents, they said, had been recommended by primary school heads not to send their children to Risinghill. Had the intake of the school, which the LCC said was a reason for closing it, been going down partly because the LCC had decided to close it? One parent, a borough councillor and market stall-keeper, said: 'We had an average of 150–200 people to our parents' meetings. At the borough council meeting, not more than ten people turned up to hear about £12 million being spent on rates on their behalf. And the LCC said that our parents' meeting did not represent parents. If I thought I could help Duane, I'd go to the end of the bloody earth for him.'

Dr Briault, the LCC director of education, who had not previously visited Risinghill, came after school to explain to the teaching staff 'the details of the reorganisation'. Not one member of the staff spoke in favour of closing the school. A week later forty-seven teachers out of sixty signed a petition:

> We, the undersigned staff of Risinghill school, deeply concerned at the grave social, emotional, educational and environmental handicaps with which so many of our children are burdened, and undeterred by the impact of those handicaps on our work as teachers, affirm our desire to continue that work at Risinghill, and mostly request the Education Committee not to close the school.'[17]

The desperate parents and staff came together to face the crisis. A staff member read out a statement which championed comprehensive education for the area but went on to suggest that 'for the sake of the children's education' Risinghill should submit to a public enquiry conducted by the Department of Education and Science.

This request for a public enquiry produced a significant exchange. Duane justified the request for an enquiry by saying: 'In the view of so much coming into light, no more harm can be done, and sensationalism may be cut out.'

Teacher (1): We must fight for the truth to come out.
Parent (1): Anything can be magnified, when the school is not compared with other schools.
Parent (2): Would a public enquiry bring more adverse publicity?
Duane: It would bring out more of the difficulties and more of the good.
Teacher (2): I've only been here less than a term. I'm concerned with the future. The LCC says the prestige of the school is going down; and therefore the school must be closed. I agree with them.
Duane: If the school closes, the work that is being done here will finish. If it goes on, it will be possible for these meetings to go on, working out the best thing to do.

In a final vote 67 were for and 49 against a public enquiry with 9 abstentions. It was also agreed that a small deputation take the demand to the DES. A resolution was passed declaring complete confidence in the headmaster and the staff, and deploring 'any action to reorganise the school or the staff'.

No enquiry was ever held. Two weeks later the LCC wrote and officially gave news of the intended closure, stating as their reason that Risinghill's intake was declining and other institutions needed its space. Only a fortnight earlier they had circulated an official document showing that the school population of London was declining and that it was their policy to keep grammar schools and single-sex schools full. When LCC officials confronted parents at a meeting to discuss the implications of the shut-down, angry parents insisted that they would appeal. On the same day, Duane wrote to Anthony Crosland, Secretary of State for Education:

The human problem presented by Risinghill has been pushed aside by the LCC but it has not disappeared and will not disappear by an administrative fiat. Before you make the irrevocable decision, come and see the school for yourself.

Whilst LCC officials were asserting that parents had been fully consulted, parents were holding another protest meeting concerning their rights under Section 76 of the Education Act 1944.

Section 68 of the Education Act was invoked, asking for the intervention of the Secretary of State for Education. A deputation of the parent/teachers' association (PTA) and the pupils discussed their points with DES officials but to no avail. Letters of support arrived at the school from other parts of Britain and also from other parts of the world. Nothing helped. On 3 June 1965 it was announced that the government had agreed to close Risinghill.

At the final prize day Duane compared his report with the 'kind you give at an inquest over a dead body, when you try to find out whether the cause of death is natural, is brought about by neglect and starvation, or is murder'. He left the conclusion to be drawn by his audience.

Risinghill died. Michael Duane, who had once said, 'I have to be in a job where I can be used and burnt out, with nothing left in reserve. This means London. London is a battlefront', was unable to secure any of the three headships which were available in Islington, and the LCC offered him a post as a peripatetic lecturer at Garnett College, London. He reflected later:

> All attempts to establish progressive forms of education have had to be made outside state systems of education. Attempts to do so within those systems have invariably resulted either in failure or in such massive modification of their aims that they cease to be progressive in any real sense. [18]

2

Hounding the heretic:
*Scottish education and
R. F. MacKenzie*

we believed in comprehensive education. We understood the
intention behind the policy and had been putting it into practice.[1]

R. F. MacKenzie: man and educator

Before the Second World War, R. F. MacKenzie had experienced
'the serene ideals' of Forest School.[2] the Forest School movement
aims to enable children's development through a relationship
with nature. The 'school' was then a base for camps where
children could explore their surroundings and enjoy learning
woodcraft skills. MacKenzie knew from this time onwards that he
wanted to extend school-time experience to include adventure;
having changed the timetable, he would then change the curriculum. The challenge was to remove all those pressures of
confinement which teachers and pupils experience whilst on
school premises. These thoughts stayed with him during the
Second World War when he was a navigator in an RAF bomber.
    As soon as the war was over, MacKenzie returned to teaching.
Had he just been a teacher who regularly organised outdoor

activities for older boys he would have stayed out of the arena of educational politics. But he chose to mount articulate criticism. He wrote letters and articles on the conflict between what Scottish school life was and what it could and should be. He asked, with characteristic directness: 'Why is it that so many educationalists, kind, intelligent, cultured and sensitive people, believe in the use of force in the classroom?' He advocated and attacked at the same time; when advocating wholly positive experience in schools he openly attacked the 'Dickens-like features of our present educational system'.

MacKenzie's battleground was Scotland:

> Scotland's schools, inflexible, lacking in self-criticism, always with the assumption of righteous indignation, blaming the pupils, unable to adapt themselves to new circumstances of living, may go the way of dinosaurs and be replaced by a totally different way of bringing up children, more flexible, more open-minded, kindlier . . . The framework of Scottish society is up for a major overhaul. [3]

The 'tawse', or belt, occupies a special place in Scottish education and is often a regular part of class routine. [4] Those who saw the tawse as an essential instrument of control were treated to some of his acid comments. Teachers were exhorted to rebel against the use of corporal punishment: 'Teachers of the world unite; you have nothing to lose but your canes.' Despite such forthright criticism, R. F. MacKenzie became a headmaster at two state schools. He chose ground on which to fight pragmatically:

> My own instinct is all against the establishment, and I feel that the only way to deal with it is to fight it. But it is possible that a less wearing, less friction-causing and ultimately more valuable way is to join it . . . and alter it from within. [5]

As a head he first tried to change the nature of state education in Scotland at Braehead Junior Secondary School. Braehead, at Buckhaven in Fife, was the equivalent of an English secondary modern. MacKenzie clashed with some prominent townspeople over the questions of examinations, sexual morality and corporal punishment. In Buckhaven his views on morals were considered 'a threat to the work of Sunday schools in the town'. This conflict was hardly surprising for MacKenzie saw inequalities and force as wrong. Rather than judge an event, he sought to understand the learning which had taken place. For example, on one school outing some pupils had been stealing. They soon admitted to their teachers that they had stolen souvenirs. After talking things over they returned the trophies. MacKenzie wrote:

> I feel the teacher handled this incident with professional distinction. The goods were returned, the shopkeeper was entirely satisfied, the pupils' respect for the bravado-cunning of shoplifters had been diluted with compassion.

In 1968 MacKenzie was appointed head of Summerhill Academy, a comprehensive school for twelve- to eighteen-year-olds in his home town of Aberdeen. The *Aberdeen Evening Express* greeted the appointment with an article whose headline read: 'Rebel Head's "Scrap Exam System" Demand'. The article referred to him as 'head of the hot-house of educational experiment, Braehead School', and reminded its readers of his previous visit to Aberdeen, when he had 'started a sensational controversy' by attacking senior secondary schooling in the city. His visit, he had said, was in order to take part in a debate in which he would make a bid 'to take education out of the middle ages'.

R. F. MacKenzie has chronicled his attempt to transform secondary schools in the books *The Sins of the Children*, *State School* and *The Unbowed Head*. Many teachers have respected and admired his writings. However, there were deep local disagreements over the man's actions as headmaster, indeed much more disagreement than there was over his attitudes as a teacher. His failings were said to be those of poor management and lack of political skills in handling his own staff. In a 1974 Open University radio programme, a Braehead teacher complained about MacKenzie's failure to hold regular staff meetings. In the same programme Douglas McIntosh (Fife's former director of education) referred to MacKenzie's lack of proper planning procedures and failure to make a clear statement of his objectives. The director held that explicit and detailed planning are prerequisites both to offset any ensuing criticisms and to provide the basis for evaluation. MacKenzie countered this argument by advocating a policy of opportunism in the curriculum whereby teachers and children could take full advantage of pursuing an educational opportunity unforeseen by the planners. He claimed 'the school curriculum should be a design for living'.

In truth, his commitments firmly inclined towards almost the opposite direction from the prevailing winds. MacKenzie's innovations in the curriculum occurred during a period when Scottish concerns centred mainly on refining the selection and examination processes. Against the background of a highly centralised educational system, MacKenzie's experiments were unique in Scotland. As an isolated innovator he was very vulnerable.

The 'academy'

Summerhill Academy was built as a showpiece junior secondary school in a predominantly working-class area of Aberdeen and opened in 1962 to accommodate about 1,000 pupils from twelve to fifteen years. Its motto was *Mens sana in corpore sano*—'A healthy mind in a healthy body'. Six years later Summerhill was restyled as a comprehensive school catering for twelve- to eighteen-year-olds.

Scottish education differs from English education in that the 'ordinary' grade of the Scottish certificate is taken after four years of secondary education and the 'higher' grade is taken after five or six years. Scottish students can take a narrower range of ordinary grade but a wider range of high grade subjects than English children.

The education committee had lavished equipment upon the school; councillors had shown a real commitment to the young:

> The builders had completed a big new four-storey building housing the physics, housecraft, chemistry, biology and geography departments, and the library. There was a games hall, a youth centre, a new bungalow for the art department, an extension of the technical department and new dining halls . . . Parents visiting the science department were astounded by the wealth of scientific equipment.[6]

Not all the facilities were fully used or worked properly but by and large such problems as existed were felt as minor irritations. In any event, examination work took first priority. The first head at Summerhill had set a tone of 'cheerful briskness' for the school with catch phrases like 'proud of its academic achievements' and 'a sense of discipline tempered with kindess'. There was a grammar school ethos which met the wishes of those working-class parents who were ambitious for their children. The impression gained is that in its first years Summerhill Academy was thought to resemble a grammar school although its higher IQs had already been creamed off and there were no pupils over fifteen.

Aberdeen Education Committee, Labour controlled, had the job of naming the school when it became comprehensive and they chose the name – 'Academy'. Psychologically, a traditional, grammar school aura continued to hang over the name; although the generic name of the school would be changed to 'comprehensive', the reality (classwork and relationships) would remain unchanged. The councillors had no experience of, or confidence in, devising alternative schemes of education.

The choice of the name 'Academy' was an omen for MacKenzie:

> It revealed the failure of Aberdeen Council to understand what comprehensive education is about and to appreciate the nature of the promise it contained. The same old examinations, the same old wielding of the belt, the same authoritarian attitudes, the same neglect of working class children; these were things forecast by this choice of name . . . No sooner was the battle for comprehensive education won that it was lost.[7]

He wrote to the local newspaper to suggest that 'We should avoid these prestigious, boastful terms – Academy, College, High School – and just say simply Summerhill School.'[8] MacKenzie became head at Summerhill in 1968. Those who appointed him knew his position and his principles.

Mr William Ross, an ex-Secretary of state, was invited to open the academy. MacKenzie was not too enthusiastic over this as Mr Ross had agreed to the closure of his previous school in Braehead. But Mr Ross chose to refer to progressive methods in glowing terms and complimented MacKenzie on his journey so far. The school newspaper had provided the foil with the following:

> In welcoming you to open this comprehensive school, we acknowledge the vision that blueprinted a new kind of school and the generosity of the local authority who made it a reality. But this is only the beginning of the story. We have a long, long way to go before Aberdeen parents outgrow the old selective senior secondary idea that ability is given only to a few. We have discovered that throughout the school population there is a wealth of ability hitherto unrecognised. It will be our job to nourish this ability and bring it to fruit.

A new approach is necessary (and that implies a reduction in corporal punishment). We see comprehensive education as an equal concern for all.[9]

Mr Ross responded by encouraging the school to 'experiment'. He drew attention to the Summerhill of A. S. Neill ('a man who brought new values to the old ideas of education') and concluded with the hope that 'Summerhill Academy will be as well known in the future for the pioneering work, for the successful work of furthering worthy ideas within Scottish education.[10] For R. F. MacKenzie it was as though 'there was a new world beginning'.[11]

MacKenzie's predecessor had acquired for the school a cottage in the countryside near the River Dee. The school ran varied activities there and school fund-raising enabled the purchase of additional transport. Summerhill Academy buzzed like a beehive in the evenings. The activities included swimming, indoor football, mountaineering training on a specially constructed training wall, canoe building, table-tennis, trampolining and badminton. In the mornings the youth wing accommodated a nursery playgroup, and the pupils helped to entertain old people on some afternoons. The many extra activities which were enjoyed led MacKenzie to conclude that when the traditional curriculum was over the school woke up.

The staff gave a lot of unpaid time to help with pupils' societies, practices and concerts. The school was recognised as being a good one for overseas visitors to see. Letters from teachers and parents all over the world arrived asking if they come come and work at, or send their children to, the school and its cottage. English educationalists communicated their interest, as did the Education Department of the University of Stirling.

During MacKenzie's time at Braehead an aluminium company had offered Inverlair Lodge free if the education committee would accept it. It would be his other school'—a 22-roomed shooting lodge at the back of the Nevis mountain range. MacKenzie had spent thirteen years negotiating the gift. The plan was to integrate Inverlair Lodge activities with classroom work at Summerhill Academy. The aim was to illustrate the truth of the maxim that 'Culture [is not] a veneer . . . but the essential food of living.' The director of education was against accepting the gift. The education committee turned the offer down. The Lodge was to have been a place of harmony, a haven in a hostile world. MacKenzie was bitter at the rejection of such a balm:

> In seeking to heal these wounds that led to violent acts, we got no support from the Scottish Education Department, nor the colleges of education nor the universities. They did not feel involved. It was one of the major problems of our civilisation but these agencies weren't giving it active concern. If we did anything other than make the traditional gesture of opposing violence to violence, we laid ourselves open to public attack, and these agencies and the Education Committee washed their hands of us.[12]

A staff divided

MacKenzie also found it difficult to introduce changes. The school had more than 1,000 pupils, and an established staff accustomed to a policy which ensured their privileges and prestige. Every proposed innovation caused a staff controversy. Some teachers maintained the 'social work' was not part of a school's function. The pupils' council was considered a challenge to the power of individual staff. A school newspaper was said to divert attention from the proper work of education. The proposal that there should be no belting of girls was not well received. All these grievances provoked angry reactions.

MacKenzie did not court his opponents. One of his prime targets was the tawse—he did not want it used 'at the discretion' of teachers or the head. Scotland's three main teachers' unions were in favour of the use of the tawse and he described them as 'reactionary associations, looking to the past and unwilling to participate in vital changes in education'.[13]

When MacKenzie tried to find the cause for the increase in the number of disruptive pupils, many teachers felt he was aligning himself with the delinquents. Eventually the education committee supported the teachers by confirming that MacKenzie was spending too much time with disruptive pupils. Unequivocally, MacKenzie attacked the teachers' unions for espousing the idea of a two-class society: 'they are part of the establishment's purpose to use the educational system to divided Society and rule'.[14]

MacKenzie's error, according to some teachers and some

Labour councillors, was in not taking tough action against recalcitrant pupil minorities. The incident which triggered the succession of events that led to MacKenzie's sacking concerned a pupil who told a teacher that he'd 'stick a knife in him'. It transpired that the pupil's mother was in hospital and he was living at home, worried about her. His dog had been ill and, although the boy had sat up with it all night, the dog had died. The following morning the boy had quarrelled with another pupil in his class. A teacher spoke sharply to him. An angry exchange followed which culminated in the pupil making the knife threat. MacKenzie tried to understand and explain the offence. Once again there was the accusation that in trying to learn from the situation MacKenzie had sided with the pupil. In the eyes of his critics he should have thoroughly belted the boy and so backed the threatened teacher to the hilt.

It was ironic that some of MacKenzie's 'best teachers' (those who gave extra help to pupils) came from outside Scotland. These teachers had confidence in the pupils. But there were also staff who believed in the old 'virtues' of corporal punishment, short hair, tidiness, school uniform, respectful manners to teachers and compliance with orders; they believed in a distance between pupil and teacher. 'In the staff a deep division underlay what seemed to be political solidarity.'[15] Moderate conservatives sided with the more authoritarian staff and began to exercise pressure on those 'in the middle'; compromise became more tenuous and the maintenance of friendly relations was in jeopardy. There were arguments over pay differentials between staff. MacKenzie was criticised both for being dictatorial when he refused to take a staff vote on whether widescale corporal punishment should be reintroduced, and for lack of leadership over other issues.

Selection procedures for staff appointments were sometimes bizarre. For the deputy headship a short list was agreed upon by the director of education. The education committee then added another name to the list and, when only three councillors turned up to interview candidates, the committee selected the one who had been added to the list even though he had less experience than the rest and supported corporal punishment. He had previously been a Labour member of the town council. His appointment was probably the turning point in the school. In a 1974 Open University television programme, MacKenzie claimed the appointment of the deputy headship was politically inspired.

From criticism to crisis

At one staff meeting MacKenzie opened the proceedings with a
short talk on school policy. He referred to the lack of consistency
in attitudes amongst staff and laid stress upon confused thinking
about discipline. He asked his teachers to be much more involved
in working out policies, making enquiries into new ideas and new
kinds of curricula. He took as his text the aphorism 'Society can
control only those who value their membership in it.' He
suggested that staff who could not work comfortably in a
progressive, more permissive climate should feel free to ask for a
transfer. His 'traditional' teachers objected to this suggestion.
Several of the 'middle of the road' heads of department said
MacKenzie polarised the staff at this meeting and strengthened
his opponents. In his own words, 'it precipitated a showdown'.[16]
He had opened up a new possibility for those who did not like his
policy; they could make *him* go.

A month after MacKenzie's policy declaration, half the staff
signed a document drawing the director of education's attention
to their concern about the school. They claimed that most
teachers, parents, pupils, institutions and other agencies—local
and outside the district—felt the policies of the school were likely
to achieve 'the continued and rapidly deteriorating situation
presently existing in many areas of the school's functioning'.[17]
Some 'areas of the school's functioning' were said to be on the
brink of collapse.

The signatories identified the central problem as one of
authority:

> so-called anti-authoritarianism is fashionable . . . the collapse of
> secular and learned authority in our society has inevitably affected
> our schools . . . It is the basic premise of this document that
> authority must exist because it is necessary for the maintenance of
> any form of pluralistic society and that this is particularly relevant
> to the specialised society of a school.[18]

There followed a report of the type of incidents causing
consternation to this 'half' of the staff; they were: apathy to work,
recalcitrance, dress, manners, obscenities, vandalism, violence,
intimidation, extortion, theft, truancy, dangerous behaviour,
unacceptable speech, lack of deference.

Having opened with the issue of authority and continued with a catalogue of offences, the document concluded with concern for the effect of MacKenzie's policy upon members of staff themselves. It hurt them 'to turn a blind eye to misdemeanours'; their status was being 'lowered'. They objected to their 'professionalism' being questioned and unrecognised'. They were 'losing heart'.

MacKenzie had, they said, 'supported pupils against teachers'; he was 'only interested in recalcitrants'; he 'discouraged use of sanctions'; he had 'denied the professionalism of a teacher who refused to accept offensive insults from pupils; he 'used the captive audience of school assembly for disseminating personal views which often went beyond his remit either as a teacher or head teacher'.

The convenor of the education committee tried to secure a consensus by asking staff members, in small groups, to work out 'a draft code of principles of conduct for pupils'. A minority did not believe that the difficulties could be settled by the imposition of a new code of rules, and this caused the main division during weeks of negotiation. Groups then met education committee representatives. Finally the officially appointed staff group presented a summary of its findings and the group chairman met a senior administrator to create a consensus. The resulting draft on school rules was a mixture of unanimous agreement on non-controversial subjects.

The first sentence of the document stated, 'It is our aim to establish a healthy climate in which learning and teaching can most effectively take place within the school community.' The preamble held that 'it is necessary to have a framework of community living which is recognised and accepted by all'. The framework was made pointedly clear in the list of 'rules for pupils': 'Do not act in a way likely to bring disrepute to yourself, to your parents or to the school.' Eight hundred working hours went into the draft. It also asserted the right of a teacher to contact the police without consulting anyone.

The education committee was pleased with the majority draft and referred to it as an agreeable consensus. For their part the committee emphasised the rule that all disruptive and disturbed children 'were to be readily identifiable'. Regular staff meetings were to be convened to 'check on the implementation of the rules'. The school council was to be 'consulted' over the new rules but also to be advised that 'the head teacher and staff agree with these rules and expect them to be observed'.

A large minority group of teachers, thirty eight in number, drew up an alternative document. The first principle according to their text was to 'regard each pupil as an individual'. They recognised that the values of the children did not necessarily coincide with those of the school, and so there could be conflicts of standards and loyalties. The minority report reasoned that:

> We should be forming small learning groups on the criteria of social, psychological and emotional need rather than on information need. Discipline, justice, right and wrong cannot be simply codified. Relevance, modification and flexibility are more important than some arbitrary and authoritatively imposed correctness. Although pupils and teachers need some form of security, a code of discipline with specified rules removes personal responsibility from the teachers. How, then, can we pretend that we are trying to promote personal responsibility in the pupil? Rules protect people from decisions they should be encouraged to make themselves.[19]

MacKenzie doubted if the staff of any other state school in Scotland had examined its function in a statement as basic as that. The minority statement was sent to the director of education and to members of the education committee. The package of documents sent to committee members also included the majority statement, histories of disturbed pupils and a headmaster's report.

The director's guidance and advice document closely mirrored the majority statement:

> In my opinion at this time Summerhill Academy lacks a basic framework of security which can only be provided by an agreed policy of procedures regulating the daily route of staff and pupils . . . In a community situation, such as a secondary school, there must be recognition of the necessary exercise of authority and acceptance of responsibility—an agreed law and order basis . . . Attempts at innovation can be almost counterproductive if they increase unease on the part of the staff. In stating my own views here I am not denying the changing nature of authority, but there must be authority which is recognised . . .
>
> Mr MacKenzie has much to contribute and he can, by leadership and positive direction, taking the staff with him, do a great deal for the community that is Summerhill Academy.[20]

MacKenzie was not invited to attend the meeting which

received these documents, and waited outside throughout. One member of the committee was the Summerhill teacher implacably opposed to MacKenzie. The education committee 'approved the recommendations of the majority staff report'.

Suspended on full pay

There followed three months of letters and meetings. The committee convenor stated that 'firm and effective leadership would have prevented this situation reaching crisis proportions'. Mr MacKenzie had shown an 'inability to be the leader of a team'; he had been guilty of 'woolly theorising'; he had not been 'sensitive to staff views'.

A massive effort was made to persuade parents to attend a meeting with the convenor of the education committee and the director. It was to be an occasion when parents could 'indicate views on various aspects of the school which they would wish to bring to the notice of the committee representatives'. Less than 200 parents came. Few participated, but criticisms of lack of discipline were made.

After a further two months the director asked for written confirmation from MacKenzie that he would implement *all* the recommendations of the majority staff report. The director wrote:

> I agree with you that the members of the Education Committee were aware of your educational philosophy when you were appointed—and they still are. Nor would I, as Director of Education, expect you to abandon your educational outlook—although it may be modified by you in the light of experience. This is not the point at issue. What is the concern and responsibility of the committee is to take such action as it deems appropriate to resolve a situation arising from the attempt to translate your aims and objectives into practice at Summerhill Academy. On this the Education Committee has made a decision. I shall be glad to have a reply in terms of the requests made in this and my previous letters.[21]

Public opinion which supported corporal punishment to 'cure' society's ills was undeniably strong. Institutions like the press, the church, and teachers' unions subscribed to it, and the education committee would have had run counter to these if it had supported Summerhill's attempt to reduce corporal punishment. An example of this attitude is illustrated by Aberdeen town council minutes recording a poll on corporal punishment in primary and special schools. Out of 8,821 respondents, 7,346 (83.28 per cent) wished retention of 'present policy'; 644 (7.30 per cent) wished progressive elimination of corporal punishment; 831 (9.42 per cent) wished immediate aboliton.

The authority's staffing committee which was convened to take 'decisive action' recommended 'the suspension of Mr Mac-Kenzie'. This recommendation went, a few days later, to the education committee. The convenor spoke of 'growing concern about the practical aspects of policy implementation at the Academy . . . a consequential disorientation of approach by the teachers individually and the eventual polarisation by significant numbers of the staff into pro- and anti-MacKenzie groups'. He claimed MacKenzie had not implemented the staff majority document and therefore had 'rendered the exercises of last autumn counterproductive'. He concluded his review with these five points;

> There is no evidence of an acceptable framework of order in the school which is necessary for the ordinary work of the school.

> There is a marked lack of respect between pupils and teachers, pupils and pupils, many teachers and pupils, and the Headmaster.

> There is confusion about the real meaning of discipline and false equating of discipline with corporal punishment.

> There is a demonstrable lack of confidence in many parents in the educational provision for their children in Summerhill Academy.

> There is a grave loss of morale among the staff. [22]

After two hours of debate, by a vote of sixteen to six, MacKenzie was suspended from duty on full pay. In March 1974, the deputy director of education, W. N. Henry, was appointed to take over the headship of Summerhill Academy.

Mr Henry set about dismantling the Summerhill Academy experiment. In June, three months after his appointment, Mr Henry held a staff meeting at which a motion was carried that the new headmaster would not be bound by the 'majority document' and then he ordered the last twenty minutes of the staff discussion struck off the record. The 'recommendations' for setting up a unit for children with problems, for increasing the number of remedial teachers, for holding staff discussions on primary–secondary liaison, for basic standards of communication, school policy and attitudes to education were not to be implemented. Monthly staff meetings decreased to one or two per term, and the venue moved from the staff room to the assembly hall. MacKenzie himself had been suspended because he had refused to accept *all* the provisions of the consensus document.

Fourteen teachers wrote to the Aberdeen daily newspaper recording their dissatisfaction at the increase of corporal punishment in the school. The director of education wrote to them suggesting they should resign. They were reported to the General Teaching Council for 'unprofessional conduct' but in the end the case was dismissed on a technicality. More stringent disciplinary measures became normal in the school, and for some months police were called in almost daily. Uniform was stressed. Latin was introduced. The school cottage beside the Dee was rarely used. 'The 'O' level grade examinations scores have gone down substantially. Attendance has also deteriorated.'[23] R. F. MacKenzie moved to make his home at a farm near Aberdeen. He was not to be a teacher or headteacher again.

There is considerable frustration in retelling the story of Summerhill Academy at such a distance and with so few sources. For whilst the immediate processes of the enquiry have been made evident, the underlying forces and longer term consequences have not. Some aspects, we feel, are missing whilst others feature as fleeting shadows. How the staff divided, the developments MacKenzie encouraged and the circumstances of his dismissal are reasonably clear. But little is known about his relationship with the local Labour Party and local teachers' unions. Neither do the parents figure strongly apart from their attributed belief that a conventional school would serve their aspirations best. Finally what seems to get lost almost entirely is that MacKenzie's purpose was to educate pupils to demand participation in government:

> It all comes back to this: you can't have an enduring political change unless it is supported by a cultural change; you can't have cultural change unless you set the schools free from their present function from being indoctrinators of the status quo. Change begins in the school, or, as Prime Minister Attlee said, in the minds of men.[24]

Surviving the stresses:
Countesthorpe College

> If you really believe as I do believe, that the development of the
> next fifty years will be to mix a central elective democracy such as
> we've got at the moment with a great increase in the rate of grass
> roots participatory democracy . . . then you've got to start it in a
> school.[1]

Tim McMullen's first headship was in 1958 at the Thomas
Bennett Comprehensive School at Crawley, Surrey. Then he
became a Principal Lecturer in Education at Coventry College of
Education. In 1966 he left Coventry to become Co-ordinating
Director of the Nuffield Resources for Learning Project. After two
years of 'accidental contact' with Leicestershire Education Authority upon the subject of 'the organisation of space within
schools' McMullen was appointed head of Countesthorpe College. The college was scheduled to open in 1970 with an intake of
fourteen- to eighteen-year-old students. McMullen was to plan
the new school and to be in post six months before it opened.

McMullen's approach to setting up a comprehensive school
had changed between 1958 and 1968. His article in *Forum*
discusses this change in terms of his strategy and his proposals for
substance:

Probably the biggest change in my thinking lies in the awareness that to design anything, a very clear definition of objectives is necessary, and that the process of deriving an organisation from a set of objectives is much aided by a 'model' to direct thinking. [2]

Furthermore:

Three main differences will, I think, mark any school I may have the fortune to control in the future: the whole academic emphasis will be on the individual learning, not the teachers teaching; the intrinsic motivation rising out of the child's curiosity, desire and achievement and creative drive will be stressed equally with the extrinsic motivation; and the school and the community will be one unit. [3]

At some points he expresses these objectives as responses to social and technological changes. At others he relates them to principles of learning:

In motivating students it is not their interests which are important but their needs. There are several implications here. First, that most learning is achieved by action, not by the passive acquisition of information; second, many aims can only be achieved by personal inter-actions such as tolerance and co-operation; third, much learning is 'caught', not 'taught', especially ethical attitudes and social behaviours; fourth, interests of individual students will be very varied; fifth, a hierarchic, authoritarian 'head-dominated' management system is an impossible framework for a school in which the authority relationships have changed between student and staff. [4]

McMullen's approach often involved combining contrasting perspectives or even potentially contradictory positions. His 'model' held specific aims like individualised learning. His 'mechanisms' were those of discussion which would make divergences and disputes manifest. In effect he was committed to getting a process under way, a process which would produce a shared policy.

We have a chance to rethink the total process of learning within a school, subject only to the demands made by outside institutions—i.e. universities and parents—and the personal and material resources available to us. This does not mean that everything we do will be different from what has been done before, but it should mean that we do not automatically repeat an established practice without considering why. [5]

In his own words, it was on this note of 'constructive disillusionment' with traditional values and practices that McMullen took up the headship of Countesthorpe College.

The formation of Countesthorpe College

In 1957, the then director of education for Leicestershire, Stewart Mason, proposed that there should be a 'limited experiment' in 'two pilot areas'. He wanted to show how secondary modern and grammar schools 'instead of driving in pairs would now drive in tandem'. To make use of existing buildings Mason proposed that all children would go to new-style secondary moderns, high or middle schools, and then all children whose parents wished them to do so would proceed to new-style 'upper' schools, the break occurring at fourteen. Parents choosing upper schools would sign a declaration promising to keep their children at school until sixteen. The remaining children would stay at the high school for a final year, or part of a year. By virtue of this reorganisation ex-grammar schools became upper school colleges. There was virtually no resistance to the plans and the eleven-plus examination was abandoned in 1959. In the creation of 'colleges' Stewart Mason had been considerably influenced by the making of village colleges in nearby Cambridgeshire.

The director also wanted the secondary schools to promote some of the primary school practices which he admired—an emphasis on individual learning and group work, interdisciplinary studies, and a flexible timetable. Stewart Mason's progressive approach in establishing community colleges centred on the design of the buildings themselves since he believed his job as an educational administrator was to build schools which would keep pace with the sought-after changes in secondary education. Over a number of years Stewart Mason had been introducing comprehensive education and many liberal innovations in 'the pocket of an arch-conservative local unit'. He did not prescribe the kind of things which people ought to do, but believed that 'individual learning is a better thing than class learning' and 'anything that moves towards a development of all the talents and interests of each individual is basically good.[6] He recognised the diffuse origins of ideas which contributed to the setting up of Countesthorpe and laid no claim to inventing them.

Countesthorpe was one of three new purpose-built community colleges and the flagship of Leicestershire's third stage of their development. It was to be built as a round wheel with the spokes of open-plan teaching areas radiating from a resources centre at the hub, and there were to be carpets throughout. The college was to be well equipped with books and with the means of making its own learning materials (offset litho and video machines). [7]

When considering the appointment of a head for Countesthorpe College, Stewart Mason said:

> Having built a school that is so obviously on the side of the trends in which education appears to be moving . . . we would be looking for somebody who was in sympathy with the changes . . . and we would very much like to have somebody who is a bit ahead. [8]

McMullen's Nuffield team members were interested in Countesthorpe College too. John D'Arcy became the first deputy head and Michael Armstrong became head of Social Studies. Tim McMullen refused to take on the traditional headmaster's authority and it was agreed that appointments and promotions would be made by groups of staff after full discussion with everyone involved. During the staff appointing process every attempt was made to recruit staff who believed in the aims of the school.

School decisions and difficulties

The twenty-five senior staff who had been appointed by April then met for a three-day residential conference to shape the curriculum. But they did so in the face of an enormous setback. For rather than becoming an upper school immediately, Countesthorpe would have to take 850 pupils, all eleven- to fourteen-year-olds, until 1973. Thus the staff would need to design a curriculum which they would have to succeed with and then quickly abandon.

There were to be four periods a day of eighty minutes each. The first two years would have a common core curriculum of four basic subjects and three interdisciplinary subjects:

Basic subjects: Maths; Science, Languages, Physical Education.

Interdisciplinary subjects: CW (Creative and expressive words, music and drama); 2D and 3D (Creative and expressive two- and three-dimensional arts and crafts, including home economics); IG (Study of the individual and group. No separate history and geography).

All pupils would have periods of independent study time. Older pupils (thirteen-plus) would be given a choice of options; they would be prepared for their participation in the 'upper school'. Guidelines on individual learning, staff—pupil relations and school management were produced.

A key decision was to constitute a 'Moot'—a weekly meeting of all staff, without a fixed chairman or formal agenda, which was to be the main legislative body in the college. Gerald Birnbaum, writing soon after the school had opened, observed that there was a very strong framework of staff democracy:

> McMullen's relationship to this body is that of chief executive and he looks upon himself as the executive agent of the Moot responsible for efficiently implementing the decisions made by the collectivity of the staff.
>
> There is an executive committee of senior staff which is responsible for more immediate decisions. The actions of the committee are of course subject to the approval and ratification of the Moot.
>
> On occasions the decisions taken by the Moot have been different from the personal views of McMullen. Already, the Moot has taken significant steps by making decisions on the nature of sanctions within the school, children's dress, the modes of address between pupils and staff. Even more important, perhaps, the Moot has overall responsibility for the appointment of new staff and the distribution of additional salary allowances.
>
> At Countesthorpe the Moot decides upon the appointment to be advertised and a committee of the staff act as the appointing body. The committee is made up of those with a special interest in the appointment, either in terms of the teaching department, or in terms of the pastoral organisation of the school. McMullen is available to the appointing committee, which can employ his experience and expertise to assist in the questioning of candidates.[9]

The Moot, therefore, was to be the vehicle for policy, and at times there could be more determination to mark a point of departure rather than agree a place of arrival. At any moment in time it would be very difficult for outsiders to fully understand the school's policy: it was simply not a fixed entity.

The college was hailed as a 'testbed for other teachers, heads and administrators who are dissatisfied with old structures, and a training-ground for students'.[10] 'Crises will blow up, as in any school—but much magnified because Countesthorpe will be working in a glare of publicity.' Publicity was inevitable with the bold claims which were being made. At the time of its opening the college was being described as 'the most advanced working model in Europe of the theories of secondary education'.[11]

The local papers responded in no mean measure to Leicestershire's plan for Countesthorpe as a 'lighthouse like no other in Europe'. The volume and intensity of newspaper reaction, however, was not anticipated. Some of the *Leicester Mercury*'s headlines read as follows:

Concept of New School Under Fire [22 May 1970].
New School is a Monstrosity [22 May 1970].
New School 'Like a Holiday Camp' [3 September 1970].[12]

McMullen forewarned his staff: 'The natural reaction to a failure will be to fall back on our previous methods and forget that these, by our own definition, are seriously flawed.[13]

The first year

The school opened in 1970 with a comprehensive intake of children from Countesthorpe itself, Leicester suburbs, an ex-city rehousing estate at South Wigston, and a few from a local children's home. It began with 850 pupils aged eleven to fourteen. It was not until October 1973 that Countesthorpe operated with its intended age range.

Major teething problems emerged. Teachers and children did not know their way around. The building was unfinished and not all the books and equipment had arrived. Innovations in curriculum based on Nuffield, Scottish and American material, BBC programmes, Project Technology, School Mathematics Project, an ICL computer course, as well as CSE and GCE syllabuses, gradually took shape. But 'gradually' is the operative word; it took a great deal of time to develop learning materials. Public relations were fraught and the *Leicester Mercury* judged difficulties worthy of regular headlines:

School's Methods to be Discussed in Public in Blaby [17 September 1970].
Parents Criticise Use of Christian Names [20 January 1971].
Local Councillor Pleads to Give New College a Chance [11 March 1971].

Tim McMullen was worried about 'whispering campaigns'. He sought to reassure parents and the public that the school was not closed to their concerns. He had been a member of a panel to answer questions on education which had been selected by the Blaby ratepayers' association. McMullen was quoted as saying that Countesthorpe College was 'not an "experimental" school- —most of the things the school was trying have been going on for fifty to sixty years'. He said that 'development' was a better word to use when referring to the school. His reported conclusion was that 'we are prepared to abandon ideas if we feel they are against the interests of the children . . . we are open-minded about how we achieve our objectives. If one thing doesn't work we will change it and try something else.' It was possibly this open-minded approach which convinced some critics that if they attacked the school vociferously enough, then action might be taken to change the kind of education with which they were taking issue. The undertaking might also have convinced them that staff were not at all sure they were doing the right thing.

There was a sense of struggling on many fronts and beginning to succeed upon some of them. An example of mixed ability grouping paying off was that of a girl whose reading age had jumped five years when she had the opportunity of working outside the remedial group. When the staff were invited to indicate which one innovation they regarded as most important, the largest single group, 45 per cent, chose 'greater equality in social relations between staff and children'. Only 11 per cent, for example, selected the 'interdisciplinary curriculum', and just 25 per cent chose 'individualised learning'.[14] The staff group had considerable experience to draw upon. Whereas 22 per cent had no previous teaching experience, 61 per cent perceived themselves as having been involved in innovations before they came to Countesthorpe, and 55 per cent in innovations in methods of teaching.[15]

Tensions within the school were those of difficult decisions and development. In May 1971 the Moot faced its most heavily charged issue so far—the question was whether or not to call in the police when dealing with stealing which had taken place within the school. The development problems were those of improving the pupils' experience, in particular to deal with 'skivers'. Teachers individually modified their programmes in the light of their first year's work and some improvements, such as providing more structure for first-year pupils, were made. However, the school council, comprising twenty-eight students and nine staff, which was the decision-making body for the social but not the academic or administrative aspects of the school, fizzled out. Some pupils, though, began to hold 'speakeasies', and staff did attend.

All in all, the school had not lost its nagging bad publicity nor had it dramatically reduced the parents' nervousness. Virginia Makins, of *The Times Educational Supplement*, returned at the end of the academic year and neatly summed up the state of play. There was, she wrote, 'an air of battle-weariness after a fairly successful engagement'.[16]

Tim McMullen was also busy in 1971 preparing another article for *Forum*[17] on the question of a school's objectives. This time his theme was of two major responses to technological society—the 'technocratic system'. The first set of aims derives from a belief in the present technocratic system, values education's place in that system, and holds to the belief that all children should have the chance to 'rise' in the system. This set of aims leads to fairly tight streaming of pupils and is directed towards examination success. The second set derives from a dissatisfaction with the technocratic system. In contrast, there is a belief that all individuals should be equally valued, that the quality of life is all-important, and that an undivided society is desirable. The outcome of this approach is non-streaming, non-authoritarian relationships, a curriculum relevant to life and participatory types of democracy. McMullen felt that the Leicestershire authority was not especially concerned with the second set of aims. He could not have automatically expected his authority's support even though his aims for the school had been spelt out at interview and in documents submitted.

McMullen's departure

As part of local government reorganisation in England, it was proposed in September 1971 that Leicester City and Leicestershire County merge administratively. Since the city had never 'gone comprehensive' — it still had the eleven-plus and two grammar schools with very good reputations — this proposal had serious political implications. The *Leicester Mercury*, aligned with city Conservatives, was highly critical of comprehensive education. Discrediting a 'radical comprehensive' such as Countesthorpe College could influence voting in the impending elections. 'Anti-comprehensive' candidates could find seats in the new council. Countesthorpe College became a political football.[18] In part, this politics was simply that of city versus county, a struggle which had little to do with electors.

By the autumn term of 1971 the *Leicester Mercury* was regularly focusing attention on the school. In December the newspaper printed a lead article entitled 'Vandalism at College', which documented severe damage to the building, including lavatory cisterns torn from walls, broken windows, stage curtains ripped and other expensive destruction. Three days later a letter appeared criticising the 'extravagant' language of the article and making a plea for objectivity. Nevertheless vandalism and the college were firmly linked as far as the news editor, Mr Simkins, was concerned.

During 1971–2, the Moot became increasingly concerned with academic and pastoral shortcomings. The core-curriculum/option system was not working as well as intended, and some children still seemed unaware of where they should be and what they should be doing. Gradually, damage and graffiti increased and provided more grist to the mill for critics.

Parental and political hostility, fanned by the *Mercury's* publicity, built up as the physical appearance of the school deteriorated. Bad publicity also affected the pupils; they faced arguments outside school hours. Some hostility could be traced to the personality and poor health of Tim McMullen, who 'disliked confrontation and appeared tense and arrogant when dealing with opposition'. In fact, he was described by the editor of *The Times Educational Supplement* as a 'buccaneer allowed to flourish in our English decentralised education system'. The implications of this image included 'administrative sloppiness and a "devil-may-care" attitude towards the public'. McMullen was largely successful in getting across the school to the national and international education world by writing, he failed in discussions with his local community.

The 'wear and tear' of so many innovations, especially with an age range younger than the school was intended for, also had its toil. McMullen had worked tirelessly at the school since his appointment but by the end of April 1971 he had been frequently absent from the school. Long absences continued until he resigned, leaving Countesthorpe in April 1972 to take a job with the Organisation for Economic Cooperation and Development in Paris.

Stewart Mason probably felt his choice of McMullen had been a mistake. He thought that McMullen had been wrong in allowing pupils to address staff by their Christian names, and should not have allowed the building to deteriorate so rapidly. Mason had 'got more than he bargained for'. He may not have appreciated McMullen's model of staff democracy and assumed that McMullen was primarily interested in democracy as a more effective, up-to-date method of achieving liberal educational goals. If so, staff democracy could have looked like a model for ducking personal responsibility. Mason's refusal to allow McMullen's wife, Marion, to teach at Countesthorpe had soured the relationship between the two men and had prompted McMullen to consider resignation even before the school opened.[19]

Tim McMullen had been determined to open a radical school and seems to have been yet further radicalised by the experience. In becoming more committed to progressive practices he grew less concerned with public reaction. He probably felt that he had become too extreme, too single-minded and determined to survive. The teaching staff were also weary of contending with critical factions outside the school. Although fortified by the excellent teacher–pupil relationships they were too busy running the school to take over a 'public relations' job as well.

Throughout the period 1970–2, Countesthorpe had been strongly supported by its governors. However, when it was necessary to appoint a new head, many staff thought that the authority and the governors would never appoint a person who would uphold the democratic organisation of the school, but they were wrong.

John Watts learns of an enquiry

The new head was to be John Watts, who had emphasised at interview that he supported McMullen's conception of the school. He was a Lecturer in Education at the Institute of Education, London, and had been head of Le Quennevais School, Jersey. Prior to that he had taught English at Sawston Village College, Cambridgeshire, and been a head of English for six years.

He was urbane and articulate, had a puckish sense of humour and firm, clear speech. His academic standing was high, he had written numerous textbooks, and he was soon to be chairman of the National Association for the Teaching of English. John Watts's public personality was very different from McMullen's. He had a 'confident and reassuring approach' and from the outset he confirmed he would work at improving the school's public relations, concentrating on co-ordination and administration. He wrote later that his role as principal was 'as the hinge in the nutcracker, a position of some strain, standing between the school, where he is accountable to the Moot, and the Administration, where he is accountable to the Local Authority and the governors'.[20]

John Watts faired well as an apologist for the school; he could speak the truth without sensationalising the difficulties. He expected conflict with the 'outside world', he wrote:

> If our objective is to assist the students to take increasing control of their own destinies, to question assumptions, to solve problems by being inventive and trained to envisage speculative alternatives, we are bound to meet conflict with an industrial society that sees schools principally as the sorting house for employment. The opposition can take various forms, from the pressure put upon Youth Employment Officers by employers, to the demands by Governors for the means of producing conformity within school: uniforms, assembly, gestures of respect and so on. In our own case, the suspicions have been directed principally at three main features: choice within curriculum, the non-authoritarian relationships of teachers and students and the participator form of government. Even among those who have looked closely enough to realise that we have not just sold out to students, that they do not do as they please, that a continuous dialogue of guidance exists, there are many who will object because the teachers are failing to dictate the fields of study, failing to instil a sense of respect for the respectable, failing to establish an institution whose

form of government implies an unquestioning obedience to authority.[21]

The dialogue among the Countesthorpe staff regarding the organisation of the school continued. Some wanted to retain the basic organisation but increase the options to cater for non-academic students; some wanted to abandon the core curriculum altogether; others wanted a total change whereby the school was broken up into 'mini-schools' with teams of teachers having total responsibility for groups of 120–150 students. 'We have neither sufficiently demonstrated to students the strength of our own commitments, values and interests, nor have we shown the strength of our own commitments, values and interests, nor have we shown sufficient regard for theirs,' wrote the group who wanted to place the pastoral system at the centre of the school's learning system. The proposals were discussed first in the spring term of 1972. From then onwards the team approach evolved. This was based on core disciplines but allowed pupils to negotiate individual timetables. The reorganisation greatly helped the school to settle down from the beginning of the third year. The success lay in the staff's commitment to make things work, in what John Watts called the 'fecundity of ideas flourishing in a situation of acceptable conflict which ensures that a critical selection ensues'. However, 'the conditions themselves improved much more speedily than local attitudes'.

Parental concern, which had built up in the initial period, culminated in the formation of a Parents' Action Committee (PAC). The PAC independently undertook a 'questionnaire survey' of parents in Blaby, Countesthorpe and Glen Parva. A meeting called by the committee's secretary, Mrs Ann Maloney, attracted 200 people, and 67 parents completed the questionnaire. These parents had a total of 95 children at the school, which at the time had a total roll of 1,200. A petition of 411 people, not all of them parents, demanded that the children should be given 'suitable and efficient education' under the 1944 Act. The publicity which the petition aroused prompted 920 parents to sign a statement expressing strong support for the staff, and deploring the sensational publicity the school had received since beginning. The first petition was welcome fuel for political opposition to the school. In the lead-up to local government reform it was clear that the debate over the reorganisation of

Leicester City schools would be a crucial issue. Countesthorpe, and to a lesser extent another 'mark 3 community college', Wreake Valley, became the prime targets.

It was in early 1973 that the group of parents critical of Countesthorpe gained the support of the local Conservative MP, John Farr. Copies of an open letter from Ann Maloney addressed to John Watts were sent in February to the *Leicester Mercury*, A. N. Fairbairn (Leicester's director of education since 1971 when Stewart Mason had retired), John Farr MP and Dr Rhodes Boyson. John Farr's call for an enquiry was taken up by Councillor Geoffrey Gibson, leader of the Conservative group on Leicestershire County Council. The charges drawn up included:

1. Staff were not up to quality.
2. Basic subjects were neglected, particularly English, Maths and Religious Education.
3. Teachers were indoctrinating students with left-wing opinions, using biased material.
4. Students suffered from lack of regular homework.
5. Sex instruction given was offensive to parents.
6. X-films were shown against parental wishes.
7. Staff had little interest in exams.
8. Leavers would have difficulty in finding anyone to employ them.
9. Students were absent to a high degree and arrived late.
10. Unrestrained violence was frequent.
11. Students were at a disadvantage from lack of a uniform.
12. Theft was rife.
13. The running of the school was in the hands of a sinister power group.
14. The college disregarded parents' wishes and the community.
15. Countesthorpe's educational philosophy of aims was contrary to approved notions.

Geoffrey Gibson received full front-page publicity and leader support from the *Leicester Mercury*. Councillor Gibson said: 'I recognise parents' concern over Countesthorpe College and we have decided there must be a public enquiry so that everything can be fully examined.' Councillor Gordon Parker, representing the Labour Party's new Leicestershire co-ordinating committee, acquiesced: 'It seems the Conservatives are sure there is something wrong with the set-up at Countesthorpe College and are quite right in that respect to initiate a public enquiry.' John

Watts, and Countesthorpe College, learned from the newspapers that there would be an enquiry.

The enquiry

Councillor Gibson announced that there would be an enquiry on 3 April 1973. The date is significant; it came in the week before the elections of a new county council. An article in *The Teacher* (13 April 1973) criticised the front-page headline in the *Leicester Mercury* for running ahead of its facts, inasmuch as the Conservative leader of the council was asking for an enquiry but the matter had not yet been officially discussed and voted upon at a full council meeting. 'Whatever the school's defects, and most schools have them, a public enquiry started by a local politician at election time is not the best remedy,' the article declared. The Parents' Action Committee, described by John Watts as 'a passing coalition of malcontents given an inflated importance recently for political reasons', welcomed the news. A spokesman for the official parents' association said, 'I do not consider that Countesthorpe should become the subject of local party politics to the detriment of our children's education.' It was not yet certain whether an enquiry would take place or, if one did, what form it would take.

On 15 June the *Leicester Mercury* urged parents to 'continue to give vigorous backing to the MP who came so uncompromisingly to their aid, and support Mr John Farr's demand for a full, open investigation'. The newspaper recognised that 'an enquiry, whatever its outcome, won't gild the Leicestershire educational lily' (22 June), but felt that 'an enquiry into one, or even two schools, would clear the air, set guidelines for the others and help to put parents' minds at rest' (28 June). A week earlier, though, the education committee had resisted pressure for an enquiry. The committee minutes record that 'in the interests of the college, pupils, staff, parents and of secondary education in the county as a whole, it is not considered desirable for a public enquiry to be held'. Nevertheless John Farr MP continued to press for an investigation and sought to have the Secretary of State for Education, Mrs Margaret Thatcher, order an independent enquiry. Councillor Nathan Harris, chairman elect of the new county education authority, thought 'that it would do no harm'.

In the event, Mrs Thatcher did not grant an independent enquiry.

A general inspection was therefore carried out in October 1973, three weeks after the cleven- to thirteen-year-old high school pupils began in their own buildings with their own head, who had taken up duties after Easter. The morale of the staff was already low and the school had suffered a major fire which affected the administration and resource areas. So when the team of HM Inspectors arrived the upper school was operating partly in temporary buildings. The composition of the HMI team gave further cause for despondency. The reporting inspector was Mr Dalgleish, chosen from another district to give the appearance of impartiality. Mr Dalgleish had, however, only weeks before transferred from Leicestershire where he had been in known disagreement with Stewart Mason and Tim McMullen. There was evidence of strong differences of opinion within the inspecting team. For example, Mr Dalgleish considered Religious Education provision did not meet 1944 Act requirements, whereas the RE inspector praised the school's programme. During the inspection itself, the staff found the majority of inspectors to be supportive and quite prepared to give helpful advice. Their interest was well founded; the 'full inspection' at Countesthorpe became what Roy Wake, a senior HMI now retired, has called the biggest in-service training course inspectors ever underwent.

The college staff and its governing body asked for the HMIs report to be published, but the DES refused. The report was ready in June 1974. The *Leicester Mercury* made selective quotations even though the report was 'confidential' and only available to politicians and governors at the time. One conclusion which could be drawn was that there had been collusion between the *Leicester Mercury* and Conservative councillors. The education committee, which had also set up a subcommittee to investigate the school further, issued a more balanced statement at a press conference. Then the chairman of the education committee invited parents to meet him and the director of education to receive their report.

At a packed meeting in the college on 19 June 1974 a summary of the inspectorate report was given by the chairman of the education committee. This was followed by an address to parents by John Watts. He referred to the 'storm cloud' which had been gathering even at the time of his arrival two years before. His position was clear:

It has been my privilege to identify with the aims and philosophy of this college, to honour the vision of Tim McMullen, his courage, his dedication to the good of our sons and daughters over the decades ahead, and to try and see those ideas translated into practice. I come, therefore, to speak not of present disaster, but of present achievement and an assured future.

Watts acknowledged that much had been attempted in 1970 with insufficient supportive preparation—which, together with an unprecedented amount of publicity, combined to make an explosive situation. He admitted that the school originally gave too few reassurances to parents. He referred to the political reasons for making an attack on the school; the reasons why the timing of the inspection was politically opportune but educationally inopportune (a comment which must have embarrassed the inspectorate).

Systematically Watts listed ten errors made and then outlined the remedies. He referred to damage, inadequate materials and finish in certain aspects of the buildings, misbehaviour, the age range of the children, co-ordination and protection of resource material, loss of books, record-keeping of students, streamlining the administrative machinery, and the implementation of too many innovations at one time. But these were errors he chose to identify, they did not correspond to John Farr's charges (see p.64). His position was this:

I pointed to errors that *had* been made. They were by no means all the school's. A principal one was to open with the wrong age group and with students in their last two terms of schooling, a decision of the LEA which was well nigh fatal and very injurious to the school and staff. It was ironic that the *Leicester Mercury* headlined 'Warden admits errors', which was what they wanted to report rather than that we had quite as much suffered from the administration's errors or politicians' errors. On the other hand, to regain public credibility, it was crucial that I admitted to errors. I wanted to be specific.[22]

Watts outlined the achievements of the school, and gave parents assurances that errors would not be repeated.

The HMI reported that they did not take issue with any of Countesthorpe's educational philosophies, but that the college

had tried out too many innovations at the same time (e.g.
management, curriculum, abolishing traditional ritual and sanctions). The staff, the majority of parents and students, the PTA,
the governing body, officers of the LEA, gave an overwhelming
expression of support for the directions in which the college was
moving, and again criticised the sensational reporting of the
Leicester Mercury.

Tim McMullen had the opportunity of delivering his own
report when, a year and a half after leaving, he gave the W. B.
Curry Lecture at the University of Exeter.[23] It is more radical than
any previous speech or writing. He argued that political action
was needed to ban the use of the educational system for selection.
This meant the ultimate outlawing of examinations, or any
substitutes such as teacher assessment or school reports, that were
designed to 'place' sixteen-year-olds either in industry or in
further stages of education. This would be the secondary school
equivalent of abolishing the eleven-plus. This view had three
underpinnings – pupils had a right to equality of education without any assumptions of where it may lead; education did not mean
middle-class values; and those who would make such a change
would have to scheme well in advance if they were going to have
far-reaching effects:

> It becomes essential that the staff provide situations, material and
> understanding for the interests commonly generated among
> working-class students; that there should be an absence of
> unnecessary regulations based on middle-class concepts of taste
> and discipline; that adults can behave so that they will be accep-
> table to such students and can themselves accept the different
> standards of speech, behaviour, and politeness. We should move
> in the direction that has been shown by 'progressive' schools, not
> because of a belief in 'progressive methods', but because they
> appear to offer the only direction which we can take to achieve
> what we really believe in . . .
>   Countesthorpe College is an attempt to build a school moving
> in these directions not based on a static blueprint, but on a
> dynamic system of participatory decisions, a school which is
> constantly trying to adjust its practices to achieve its aims. Though
> it is early days and despite outside pressure from press and politi-
> cians, it is showing that a viable school based on these principles
> can be developed.[24]

Aspects of survival

John Watts maintains that it would have been difficult to carry on without local, national and international support. One irony of the story, as Virginia Makins observed, was that it was the only traditional element left in the management of the school—the governing body—that saved the original conception from defeat. Countesthorpe College was lucky in having a supportive governing body, particularly with regard to Dr Geoffrey Taylor, its chairman. Dr Taylor's three children have attended Countesthorpe over a ten-year period and two have gone on to Cambridge to read Medicine. Dr Taylor has been at Countesthorpe longer than any of his children. During that time no compromise has been made on Tim McMullen's plans for a school run on the basis of participatory democracy, and the school has settled down with its intended age range.

The school has succeeded in establishing the means whereby children learn more and become more autonomous. Many critics have suspended judgement or retracted their criticisms in the light of the relatively smooth running of the school. Countesthorpe College's determination to give students the examinations at sixteen-plus which they need, but no more, has given a favourable pass rate compared with other schools in the county, whether comprehensive or selective.

Watts claims the school is not a blueprint, but 'an example that alternatives are possible; that students and assistant teachers can themselves generate and maintain change without dependence on initiatives from above and without'. He adds the caution that the Countesthorpe approach can only be adopted by other schools if a local authority is supportive and if the staff are eager to subscribe to the objectives and responsibilities which follow from participatory government.

Countesthorpe survived and then struggled to overcome its problems. By 1977 John Watts edited the published book *The Countesthorpe Experience* in which the perspectives of pupils, parents, staff and visitors make a kaleidoscope of firm claims for its structure, culture and processes. Countesthorpe College too, no doubt, provided Watts with the inspiration for the new covenants for students, teachers and parents he proposed in *Towards an Open School*.[25] In 1980 Watts left Countesthorpe and was later to become responsible for in-service training for head teachers in the Wessex authorities.

Part two

Sutton Centre through the 1970s

4

Before the trials:
Sutton Centre's early years

the school community should come together to build a new democratic society where real social justice, real equality of opportunity and real living are found [Stewart Wilson].[1]

Stewart Wilson's commitment to the community school

Stewart Wilson entered teaching in 1958 after a spell in the Royal Navy and industry. He had graduated in Geography at his native Aberdeen University and been a submarine officer. He then held a rapid succession of senior posts in secondary modern and grammar schools, including being head of department at Rushcliffe Grammar School, Nottingham. His first headship was at Staplyton, Teesside, in 1966. Here he challenged his staff and the education authority to dispense with unnecessary trappings and take on fresh tasks:

The main job is to remove all the artificial barriers which have been created over the years in the world of education (for any

school which has aspirations to be a real community school).
These barriers are many-fold:

1. the barrier we have put up around our educational buildings, our
   schools if you like.
2. the barrier which we have put up to other sections of the
   community.
3. the barrier which we have erected around ourselves as teachers
   with regard to our teaching role.
4. the barrier with which we have surrounded the curriculum of
   the school and the subject syllabuses.
5. the barrier we have put up around the young people in our
   schools as though they become different animals once they step
   inside the school.
6. the barriers which often exist between a Head and his staff and
   between different departments in the school. [2]

A conference of teachers at Hartlepool in November 1972 had
these barriers described and then heard them verbally demolished. The conference had been called prior to comprehensivisation in the town. Stewart Wilson took the opportunity of
advocating its 'logical development into community education': [3]

And what about the biggest barrier of all—our professional
training which tell us that we are equipped to teach young
people between the ages of eleven and sixteen in a building which
shall be called a school. Isn't the community our classroom?
Couldn't much of our drama and singing and painting and photography, for example, take place in the bus station or the supermarket or the police record office or the town hall computer
department? Isn't the living community the real starting and
finishing point for our science and geography, history and environmental studies teaching? Isn't this the real world which our pupils
should be looking at and listening to and thinking about? And
isn't this the way to interest the outsider, the man-in-the-street, in
education? [4]

Wilson was going much further than proposing technical
reforms; he linked his campaigns together to form a crusade. He
attracted attention because he had shared with Staplyton's staff a
vision of wanting to be teachers in a community school. Having
been an 'arden advocate' of comprehensive education in the
1960s his campaigns had now developed to include:

the common system of examining at 16+; mixed ability teaching;
block timetabling; the opening of educational premises for 360

days a year; joint adult and student classes—and the abolition of corporal punishment.[5]

His commitment, campaigns and success at Staplyton made him a notable figure. He could speak at Hartlepool with some independence, too, for he knew then he was to become the first head at Sutton Centre in January 1973.

Sutton Centre's beginnings

In September 1970 senior officers of Nottinghamshire County Council met the development committee of the Sutton Urban District Council to discuss the possibility of an educational and recreational complex in the town centre of Sutton-in-Ashfield. It was agreed to commission a feasibility study. There was great urgency, because the raising of the school leaving age would make the town's older, small secondary schools completely inadequate. There was an immediate need to build a comprehensive school for 1,200 pupils. It was also desirable to provide leisure amenities which would enliven the mining and hosiery town. These hitherto staple industries would experience serious decline before long and new industries needed to be attracted to the area.

The feasibility study was carried out in the winter of 1970—1. A group of chief officers of the county council interviewed a great many people in the area and what emerged was that the town, as such, was lacking in focus. Like a wheel without a hub, it was fragmented. 'There's nowt to do in Sutton,' as one young man said. The chief education officer and county architect developed the notion of a community school in a community centre. They proposed combining leisure centre, youth services, teachers' centre, careers office, day centre for the elderly and handicapped, LEA adult education, Workers' Educational Association/ university extra-mural and adult literacy with statutory education—thereby mixing adult and child education. They also proposed including new office accommodation for area social service, probation and the registrar of births, marriages and deaths. The proposed school would be one substantial part in a much larger and varied whole.

The notion of a community school was by no means original, but the combination of the school in a leisure and amenity centre, adjacent to a shopping precinct and a market place, was a unique idea. The essential consequence for pupils' learning was clearly stated in the feasibility study: 'If education in school is to be preparation for life, we see no fundamental difference between education and social education.'[6] The officers ended their study on an optimistic and idealistic note:

> The general conclusion which was drawn from these wider investigations (with both County Officials as well as groups and individuals in Sutton) is that the concept of a more fully integrated community provision is now widely accepted, not only in many parts of this country but also in Europe. We consider that this thinking is sound. It makes financial sense because it saves wasteful duplication of buildings provided at great public expense. It makes social sense because it does much to bring back into purposeful community activity many groups of people who have in more recent years gone their separate ways; because it enriches, as no other social agency can enrich, the whole texture of community living. In the narrower sense of the word 'educational' it makes educational sense, because it enables us to draw our schools out of their traditional seclusion and to bring them into the market place, where they will be better placed to provide that preparation for real life which education ought to be, and which it has often not been in the past.

This concept was attractive both to educationalists and to architects. The county architect of Nottinghamshire, who designed the centre, when speaking about Henry Morris ('the "only begetter' of the community school'), said: 'It fascinates me that he spoke at the RIBA in 1956 on community schools and no one really heard what he was saying. And now, suddenly, for a variety of reasons, here it all starts up as if he were still alive.' The plan of construction was stretched out into phases beginning with the school teaching areas and ending with offices.

Local government reorganisation was imminent for both Sutton Urban District Council and Nottinghamshire County Council. The new-found partners pressed ahead by agreeing to expenditure and creating a management structure:

> we would recommend the creation of two bodies—the Governing Body of the School, with responsibility for the affairs of the school proper and for adult education classes, and a Management Committee responsible for the recreational aspects of the Centre with representation from the various interests involved. The spheres of

responsibility of the two would obviously overlap in places and there would be advantage in some cross-representation.

An overall management council of six to eight members was proposed. The school governing body was a statutory require-ment; and the recreation management committee would oversee public use of the recreation facilities during evenings, weekends and school holidays, having representatives from the Sutton UDC and the county council. The management council would be a unique body with interests ranging from public participation to the welfare of the many minorities also housed in the centre. But there was no insistence from either side that the management council be formed. They were, after all, both embroiled in elections and reorganisation. Sutton Urban District Council was merged with the administration of two other towns to form Ashfield District Council. Both Ashfield and Nottinghamshire councils were Labour controlled after the elections with the active opposition of the 'Ratepayers' in Ashfield and Conserva-tives at County Hall.

Sutton Centre 1973 – 7

Between January and April 1973, Stewart Wilson had recruited thirteen senior staff. As they had not yet moved to Sutton Centre he sent them questionnaires on all aspects of school life. It was difficult to make replies whilst holding down a job. It was also awkward to sort out the replies. So a weekend conference was held at Staplyton's field centre in Yorkshire to agree broad principles: 'the school is represented as Sutton Centre and not as Sutton Town Centre Comprehensive School'.[7]

There would be a common curriculum of eleven areas:

Basic Skills.
Communication and Resources.
Creative Arts.
Environmental Studies.
European Studies.
Home Management.
Literature and Drama.
Mathematics.
Personal Relationships and Community Service.
Science.

Sports and Leisure.
Technical Studies.

The purpose of this curriculum was to develop pupils' abilities. The Communications and Resources department, for example, described their aims as to help all pupils be mature citizens in the following ways:

Critical, reasonable, able to find resources in community and personal experience.
Responsible, self-disciplined in behaviour and tasks.
Responsive to the needs of others, to the effect of self on others and working with others and in larger groups.
Articulate and expressive, rational in argument, able to decide between alternatives.
Creative and able to derive pleasure from aesthetic activity, music, art, sport and media.
Confident.
Aware of community life, opportunities in the community as well as needs and responsibilities in the community.
Aware of the family in family life and the community.[8]

There would be no setting or streaming or preparation for 'O' levels. All pupils would work towards Mode III CSE. The staff were expecting the common sixteen-plus examination to be introduced in a matter of years; by the time their first fifth formers were put to the test they thought that common examinations would have been established.

The second element in the framework was the operation of a simple and flexible timetable. The week was divided into ten blocks of time; five morning and five afternoon sessions. Nine studies were to be weekly whilst Basic Skills and Communications and Resources required 'withdrawal' for longer periods. The tenth session each week was left free for the pupil to choose which study to develop further. Adults could choose to attend any class without prior notice. The block timetable meant that there was no need to ring bells and release streams of children on to throughways. This, it was felt, would make it more possible for adults to join classes. The voluntary principle was extended still further by the development of 'eleventh sessions'; these were to be held in the evening between 6.30–8.30 when children and adults could come into the school to pursue both vocational and recreational interests.

The block timetable was an immense asset in reducing the institutional atmosphere of the school. It also prepared the way for suspended weeks; weeks when the whole school timetable was transformed and week-long special-interest projects would be offered by staff either individually or in teams.

The third element was a tutor group system of mixed ability teaching. The aim was that, allowing for a few alterations in the first or second year, the tutor group should be constant throughout the school career of each student and should be both the social and academic unit of school organisation—the group and their tutor would remain the same for five years. This stability, coupled with the home visit principle that tutors should visit the families of their group twice a year at least, was intended to create a situation of developing relationships. Each student and teacher would have an identity and responsibility, not merely as an individual with certain abilities in certain subjects, but within a group, and with a particular area of the school. The tutor was to spend the first half-hour with the group every morning. One of their first projects was to make displays for their 'area'. During the rest of the day other groups would use it and during the evenings and weekends the area could be used by adults in classes or in meetings.

Initially the 'eleventh sessions' were entirley voluntary and in additior to a full teaching load. Block timetabling and the giving up of free sessions meant that the tutor group size could be kept at twenty-four pupils and so help mixed ability teaching. Parts of the framework rested upon other parts, all fitting together to create the school culture as it grew to its full complement of pupils and staff. It was possible for Stewart Wilson to present a united front to parents in a strikingly confident manner:

1. My staff and I are concerned about all boys and girls at Sutton Centre, the able, the average and the least able.
2. We are determined to see our able boys and girls take a subject as far as they can, which in many cases will mean 'A' level and scholarship level in our sixth form as it develops during the next four years.
3. We are equally determined that no boy or girl shall see themselves as rejects because they are not very clever at their various school subjects.
4. Above all we are determined that, with the back-up of our student profile, employers and colleges will be given the fullest

possible information about our boys and girls so that it is not only their abilities in a particular subject which are recorded but also their qualities as people.[9]

The director of education publicly commended their basic principles. In an article about Sutton Centre published in 1975 he wrote:

education is the process of learning to live rather than the elite learning to pass examinations; this is not an activity reserved for school hours but one that goes on at all times and at all places where people widen their experience.[10]

After a year's trial period with eleventh sessions he had been persuaded to support the initiative with a 10 per cent staffing allowance. But the director, no matter how strongly committed, could not support the school in every way. For one of Sutton Centre's phases, the lower school, was put back to being Phase four. The completion of the school would have to come after the building of another comprehensive. Only three months after arriving, the new staff learned that the school would not be finished until at least 1979; the amalgamation with two old secondary moderns would continue anyway and these annexes would remain open until the building programme was completed.

Sutton Centre 1973 – 7: staff, pupils and parents

When Sutton Centre opened as a school in September 1972 its intake was 300 pupils. The majority of these came from Huthwaite, a mining village near Sutton, and they had all passed the last eleven-plus examination to be taken in the area. They were joined by 'difficult' pupils referred by other schools, one primary school class and the children of teaching staff. Each year, four 'feeder' primary schools in a set area sent their oldest pupils, and parents from further afield applied to have their children admitted. More than a quarter of the pupils were eligible for free school meals.[11]

The Centre had proved popular. Each tutor group elected a representative to the school council which met weekly during 'tutor time'. The school council had drawn up a 'code of conduct' and then agreed it with the head. Clause one read: 'Everyone in the Centre is asked to show consideration for others.' Guidelines for clothing were discussed in preference to there being a uniform. Weekly, in the *Sutton Centre Bulletin*, the attendance of each tutor group was published as a percentage and graded from 'excellent' to 'needing attention'. The average for the year 1976–7 was 90.8 per cent attendance. Ninety per cent was considered the target whatever the reason for absence. Those tutor groups with 95 per cent or more attendance were commended with a special mention in the *Bulletin*. A league table of times in the charts was published and those down in the basement were chided. One-hundred-percenters were nominally members of a club. Once a fortnight the headmaster officially visited the tutor area to assess its cleanliness and colourfulness: 'Keep Sutton Centre tidy' had virtually become part of the curriculum. It was this personal pride and shared effort that was said to be the reason for there being so little vandalism of any kind.

Attendance at eleventh sessions was recorded in a register. Adults paid 60p a session in 1976–7 and other schools' pupils attended free. During 1976–7 there were 62 eleventh sessions with attendances that amounted to:

Sutton Centre pupils	11,786
Adults	2,258
Visiting pupils	241

Mathematics was the most popular 'taught' session, running five nights a week with at least two tutors. Even in the depths of winter there were never less than forty pupils a night. The library was popular throughout the week. The average each night did not fall below sixty children. Of the 1,658 library attendances of boys 45 per cent were those in the fourth year. Of the 1,501 library attendances of girls 43 per cent were those in the fourth year. The proportion shows that preparation for CSE work was a powerful incentive to use the library. The library was well lit and heated whereas many of the children's homes were not so well endowed.

In 1975–6 the school had, in round figures, 700 pupils; in 1976–7 there were 900. More staff had joined and only five had left in four years. Three of the five left because of pregnancy or promotion of spouse. In 1976 there were over 400 applications for eleven Scale One posts; young and enthusiastic teachers were prepared to move from all over the country. In practice continuity of staff was secured by the recruitment policy which deliberately encouraged probationers to join. Many of these had already worked as student teachers on placement, were known to the staff and were committed to the philosophy of the school.

Thus, as the school gradually built up in size from 300 in September 1972 to 900 in June 1977, the staff, although increasing from thirteen to sixty-four, retained a commitment to the community school idea and to the approaches worked out in weekly staff meetings. The principle of rotating chairmanship had been introduced. An agenda sub-committee, with a representative from each department, set the topics for discussion and so the meeting was as open as staff wanted it to be. Technicians, clerks and cleaners came to the staff meetings too. Some of these workers, like some of the teachers, were also parents.

Parents of Sutton Centre children were largely employed in hosiery, engineering or mining, 80 per cent of them as operatives. It is not surprising to find traditional attitudes to education amongst Sutton people. The majority of jobs available for school leavers do not require qualifications and are often secured by family influence. Education has in one sense, therefore, a limited relevance as an experience rather than as the promise of attainments. The school, despite its innovations, in general secured the parents' approval. Evidence supporting this view came from a survey carried out by Elsey and Thomas with a WEA class. They found that there was active involvement by parents in a range of activities and functions within the centre and home–school relationships were rated as being very good. They also found that 'a main source of discontent appeared to come from proponents of more traditionally conceived methods of education; suspicious of the integrated curriculum and of the common CSE examination system'. [12]

The school's open-door policy and its central location did allow full scope for critics. One of the parents who was to lead the campaign against the school had heard Stewart Wilson speaking to parents at his daughter's junior school. He felt anxious then, particularly over the Centre's commitment to CSEs rather than 'O' levels, which he saw as handicapping children when it came to securing jobs. he said that 'it was all very well for Wilson to assure parents that he had consulted firms in the area and that they had expressed willingness to accept the idea of a profile plus performance in Mode III CSE, but in reality, in a competition between pupils with 'O' levels and those without, the Sutton children would be the losers'. He had met his daughter's tutor when she first started at Sutton and had built up a good relationship with him. He had accepted the invitation to go into the school and see for himself but had been upset by 'the level of noise'. He had gone on a camping trip with the tutor and a group of pupils but had been alarmed by the informality of both dress and speech.

In contrast, one of the parent governors spoke of the way in which the Centre had changed his life and brought him much closer to his family: 'Because we did so many more things together. I stood for parent governor because I wanted to give something back.' At the election there were nineteen parents as candidates for the parent governorships. This was the same May 1977 election which returned the Conservatives to power at Nottinghamshire's County Hall.

The school in the Centre

There was no insistence on the part of either Ashfield District Council or Nottinghamshire County Council that the management council should meet; and it never did. In time, the two were to see themselves as the proprietors of different parts of the same building despite the fact that there were 'various other interests' to be considered.

Whereas the headmaster was responsible to a governing body and beyond to the county council, the recreation manager's position was peculiar in that his management committee was not accountable to any formal body within the district council even though he and his staff were direct employees of the district council. The headmaster and recreation manager were to have equal but different statuses,[13] whilst the Centre as a whole was to have no overall management. The recreation manager was appointed in 1975 and then had two years in which to specify the staff he required and the atmosphere he wished to create.

The feasibility study had assumed that the school, the leisure centre and all other parts would work from common principles. It also hoped that the school would be operating from September 1973 and the Centre as a whole from September 1974. But there were big problems. The urban district council and the county council had had to refer a disagreement over fire regulations to the Secretary of State for the Environment. Their differences were over fire regulations in schools and public buildings. The regulations state 'fire break periods', i.e. the time estimated for a fire to spread from one part of the building to another. Children, because they are said to know their way around, are 'allowed' less fire break time, whereas the public using the Centre would need longer. As a result, fire doors had to be resited and ceilings replaced at a cost of £38.000. This work was delayed by disputes between officials. The relationship between county council and urban district council became less than cordial.

The recreation manager spoke of a 'family leisure centre'. At a local conference in January 1977 he spelled out his differences from the headmaster of Sutton Centre in terms of 'monitoring and controls'. There would be no agreement between them over a policy to decide how 'open' the Centre should be. His 'section' was not going to be 'lax'.

The leisure facilities had been finished and available for use a year before they were officially open to the public in February 1977. The fire regulations work within the school was still taking place six months after the leisure facilities were opened. The struggle between the UDC and the CC had affected them both and made it most unlikely that agreement would ever be reached over the formation of a management council. Indeed, as the complex developed (the staff of the school increased to sixty four and the recreation staff to fifty seven in May 1977) it became more clear that they were governed by different attitudes towards ways of working, particularly with school children.

In the leisure centre there was a supervisor and four leisure attendants on duty from 7.30 every morning. They and the teachers represented very different kinds of authority. The attendants wore uniform, worked shifts and had no training for dealing with children. The teachers, with their informal style and the non-authoritarian discipline methods of Sutton Centre school, had close personal relationships with the children. Not surprisingly conflicts arose over the question of discipline. Worse still, the attendants had very little to attend to apart from the three squash courts, the bowls hall and a third of the ice-rink; the rest of the leisure centre was, in fact, the school during school time. Within weeks there was talk of legal action between the headmaster and the recreation manager. The latter chose to issue memoranda rather than meet people face to face.

Battle-lines, so recently drawn, hardened to entrenched positions.

Through the Sutton Centre Users' Association, a body which stood outside the existing management and acted as a pressure group, the recreation manager and the management committee had been under pressure to open from November 1976 onwards. Criticism then increased. Within two months of opening the leisure centre facilities, a ruling was made by the management committee, on the advice of the recreation manager. The rule was that under-eighteen-year-old spectators should no longer be allowed in the recreation area during public time, even if they were Sutton Centre pupils. This ruling was the exact opposite of the school's policy for the Centre as a whole. For nearly four years the school had been calling itself the Centre and proclaiming that it was open to all, at any time.

Stewart Wilson was heartily sickened and amazed that such rulings could happen at all. He made up his mind and spoke forthrightly:

> Joint management is doomed to failure because with the best will in the world, if you get two or more people running a Centre like Sutton Centre (we have nine separate heads in Sutton Centre with two others, the Building Superintendent and Catering Manager, answerable, varyingly, to all nine) the chances of their always agreeing on fundamental matters of principle and philosophy are negligible . . . And even if the individuals on the management team agree, the chances of their parent bodies agreeing are even more remote . . . The public in Sutton were denied access to our magnificent recreation facilities for over a year because the District Council wouldn't see eye to eye with the County Council over fire regulations and the handicapped people were penned back into their Day Care Centre by a Social Services Committee which no doubt wished to demonstrate its muscle on the pretext that a building which their people had been using for over a year had suddenly become a high fire risk.[14]

These setbacks were hard to take but there were also practical problems to be solved. The reorganisation/ amalgamation/ reopening as annexes was scheduled in September 1977. The respective schools' staffs, Eastbourne and Westbourne, had to be interviewed, and some at least had to be given jobs at Sutton Centre. There were equipment, bussing, tutors' group areas and timetables to sort out. For in September, for the time being,

Sutton Centre was going to be a split-site comprehensive with one site in a community centre over which there was neither agreement nor control. The school size would jump from 900 to 1,500 and some new staff would be the old staff of the older annexes back on their own territories. For the first term of the new year it looked like a matter of literally holding your breath.

5

A term of incidents:
October to Christmas 1977

The way of life of the school had stretched people to the limits, and they were now being stretched further by new necessities. Amalgamation brought so many practical problems. Only the first-year students would have all their teaching at Sutton Centre. The remainder would sometimes be 'bussed'. For teachers, travelling would be more difficult as they would have their tutor groups in one building and their teaching sessions in another. Theoretically there was no time allowed between tutor group sessions and teaching sessions. Teachers dashed by bicycle and car. Needless to say they resented the pressure. They parked where they could and often on yellow lines. There was some mutual obstruction with the doctors at the adjacent health centre, and there were £6 fine notices to be negotiated.

Eastbourne and Westbourne schools were further problems in themselves. Eastbourne looked as if it had been a private house built in late Georgian times. Around it there were the wooden sheds of a gymnasium and a classroom block. It had an air of faded grandeur; more faded perhaps because the building was beginning to crumble and did not look as if it had been the product of first-class craftmanship. Eastbourne is on Station Road, which is 'established' Sutton. On the left are prewar council houses, beyond the junction on the right are prewar private semi-detached. 'Aristocrats of labour' on the left, 'Aristocrats of labour' on the right; the quiet, soft-spoken 'respectables'.

Westbourne was also an older school, the forbidding Victorian Gothic kind. It looked, every inch of dark red brick, huge rectanges of small white-rimmed windows and hard ribbons of mortar, like a secondary modern school. It is on the Huthwaite Road, a road of 1930s mock-Tudor substance with new postwar council and private housing behind. The workers of Westbourne's neighbourhood had jobs similar to those of Station Road but they were later arrivals, and may have been less secure, their respectability quite simply being less established.

Westbourne and Eastbourne were both buildings where the ethos of Sutton Centre would be resisted by the very look and feel of the buildings themselves. Both schools (as silent teachers) held very little to encourage day-to-day parental and voluntary group involvement. Two contrasting neighbourhoods, too: a new class dimension for Sutton Centre. The aspiring workers for whom Westbourne had been conspicuously successful were being told to abandon the careful programming of Westbourne in favour of what looked like the pot-luck of Sutton Centre. They were anxious and often outright hostile and had been so for months. They wanted the spirit and substance of Westbourne to live on within Sutton Centre. Under pressure, senior Sutton Centre staff agreed to Westbourne pupils remaining together in tutor groups.

The incident which led to the enquiry was a lesson for a tutor group of third-year pupils newly arrived from Westbourne Secondary Modern School.

Monday 17 October 1977

On Monday 17 October a teacher in the Personal Relationships and Community Service course began his lesson by asking the question, 'Why do people swear?' There followed a series of questions—'What do you mean by swearing?' 'Why do some swear words offend more than others?' 'Is it the word, or is it the way it is said?' 'Does it make any difference who is swearing?' 'What may prevent you from swearing?' 'What standards do you expect in friends of the opposite sex, older family, younger brothers or sisters, your own children or yourself?'

The children responded by giving examples of offensive swear words; listing proper names and 'slang' names. One thirteen-year-old girl made notes under the headings 'misused words', 'slang words', 'companion words', 'blasphemy words', and 'reasons for not swearing'. she took the notes straight to her mother at dinner time. Her mother, the manageress of a launderette close to the school, was shocked and showed the notes to some customers in her shop.

During her own lunch break she discussed her daughter's lesson with her husband and they decided to go and see the teacher concerned. An appointment was quickly made and they both met the head of department and the class teacher the following day. The mother believed that they spoke to her about some people having Victorian morals, being prudes and strait-laced. She thought they meant her; she said later: 'They told me I had Victorian standards!' She contacted her husband's GP who was also a ratepayers' association district councillor, a member of the joint sports centre's management commitee and the day centre's advisory committee. They did not know that he was also a recently appointed governor of the school—and he did not tell them either. Councillor Stein advised them that they should call a meeting of all the parents from their daughter's class. He put them in touch with a Conservative County Councillor and a meeting was suggested for 25 October.

The same afternoon of the visit from the two parents the teacher and his head of department told Stewart Wilson what had happened. He wrote to the parents straight away and included the following sentence: 'I understand you have some grievance or complaints against Sutton Centre; may I respectfully suggest you discuss them with me, rather than broad-cast them around your launderette to all and sundry. Some of your statements, I understand, are bordering on slanderous.'

This letter outraged the mother. She already felt angry that the teacher and his head of department had implied that the problem was her own 'Victorian attitude to sex'. She objected strongly to her daughter being taught swear words and indeed 'wrong words'. She accepted that the purpose of the lesson was to discuss with the children the reasons for swearing but she and her husband felt that in doing so their daughter would be encouraged to learn words of which she had previously been unaware.

On Friday 25 October there was a meeting involving thirty one parents (twenty of whom were couples). They met in Dr Stein's house. Dr Stein was there together with county councillor Radford and a petition was drawn up expressing the concern that the parents felt. The petition read:

> We the undersigned deplore teaching pupils at Sutton Centre the meanings of swear words and slang words. We feel that this can only result in an increased use of these words by pupils and a decrease in moral standards.

It was agreed to form a parents' action group. On the advice of Councillor Radford the parents decided that the petition should be sent directly to the chief executive officer, Mr O'Brien, rather than to the director of education, or indeed to the chairman of the board of governors. The parents, in interview, insisted that the director of education had ignored parents' previous complaints about the school. They were advised that it would be perfectly proper to go above and directly to the chief executive officer. Along with the petition the parents sent a letter asking for a meeting with the chief executive officer.

Gathering clouds

Between 25 October, when the petition was signed by the thirty one parents and sent to Nottinghamshire County Hall, and 21 November, when the meeting between the Parents' Action Group and the chief executive took place, further incidents occurred. The school was twice page-one news in the *Notts Free Press*, Sutton's own old establish paper,[1] although neither report mentioned an action group or swearing.

On 4 November the *Notts Free Press* carried the headline: 'Mothers Storm Out of Punch and Judy Show'. The previous Saturday, children from the Centre had been giving a free public performance in the library theatre. Two mothers with very young children walked out of the performance. A controversy followed on the letters page of the *Notts Free Press*. The two women defended themselves whilst parents and pupils from the school said it was an enjoyable and worthwhile production and not frightening at all. To the drama teacher and head it was an incomprehensible attack upon the school.

Next came a protest from the chairman of the Sutton Chamber of Trade over the selling of jewellery at the Centre as a fund-raiser. The chairman, Councillor Tagg, who was also leader of the ratepayers' association, said that such sales were unfair and detrimental to the interests of Sutton's shopkeepers. The school felt these attacks as irritants, as shots across the bows intended to warn them that its activities were not approved of. However, there is another way of looking at these incidents—they can be seen as 'shots in the air', as a call to arms for the school critics.

The incidents were seen by members of the parents' action group as an indication that Sutton Centre was in trouble, not only with parents, but also with the Sutton community as a whole. It encouraged them to collect further allegations about the school. By the time the County Hall meeting took place, the swearing lesson was no longer the only offence, though it was still being discussed as the indisputable cause of complaint.

One parent claimed that he had kept a child away from school for three or four months and yet 'no one had chased the matter up'. Another repeated his claim that CSEs were not as acceptable as 'O' levels to local employers despite Stewart Wilson's reassurances to the contrary; also, on 16 November his daughter had been involved in a fight with another girl and he insisted that no action had been taken by the school, despite the fact that the fight had been recorded in the police station. The fight—a rare incident at Sutton—had been over a boy outside the youth service coffee bar. Stewart Wilson's own daughter was taking an 'A' level at another comprehensive school in Sutton. This was said to indicate that he was giving her preferential treatment.

Furthermore, the parents' action group said, a homosexual who had previously been convicted for assault, and was at that time on another charge of homosexual assault, had just been employed at the school as a caretaker. They believed he had been taken into employment with the full awareness of the headmaster. This was not strictly true; the post had been difficult to fill and he had been engaged without his references being taken up. The headmaster, nevertheless, did not sack him or redeploy him when he was told of the parents' concern.

These allegations and the parents' petition were the agenda of the meeting on 21 November with the leader of the county council, the education chairman, the chief executive officer, the chairman of the school governors and the director of education.

The headmaster was not invited, and the shopkeeper and launderette-manager parents were surprised at not finding him there. The parents were offered an enquiry. What is more, they were offered an independent enquiry into the school and promised that the homosexual caretaker would be sacked.

Throughout this period, from 17 October to 21 November, no hint of the parents' petition or allegations against the school came to the notice of the press. The chief executive officer, Mr O'Brien, had advised parents not to speak to the media. However, after their meeting the *Nottingham Evening Post* did carry the first story of the swearing lesson. The parents' action group could not conceal their triumph, and had tipped off the *Evening Post*.

The promise to hold an 'independent', i.e. not an official HMI, enquiry into the school was made by the chairman of the county council. But the responses of the school, the parent and staff governors and the teachers' unions to the enquiry decision were all to affect the nature of the enquiry itself.

The head's reaction

Wilson was summoned to Nottinghamshire County Hall on 25 November and was told that there would be an independent enquiry into his school. He was not to speak again to the press. On the 21st his reaction to the press had been to try to play down the significance of the parents' petition over the swearing incident and defend the teacher involved. At the meeting on the 25th, however, he realised the seriousness of the situation, when the director of education stayed silently taking notes throughout the meeting. Wilson was that night to address a regular parents' meeting upon the curriculum at Sutton Centre. He took the opportunity to explain that the school was to be 'enquired into' by a special project group. The parents' action group were not present, having been advised by County Hall not to attend. It was an emotional meeting at which parent after parent testified to their appreciation of the school's effect on their children and their family life. Stewart Wilson promised to stand firm and maintain the innovations that had come to mean so much to parents.

The staff response was organised initially through the three staff governors. They convened a joint meeting of staff and parent governors along with the two Labour councillors who were still on the new governing body. They all met together the following Monday. With the exception of the Conservative councillors and Dr Stein it was a full governors' meeting. Together they protested at the chief executive's decision to cancel the first governors' meeting and demanded that one be held as soon as possible.

At the two staff meetings held that week a letter was written to the director of education and the county council leader. The letter asked for specific charges to be stated, demanded 'due process' and protested at the ambiguous position of some of their governors.

The staff meeting on 30 November coincided with the appearance on page three of the *Sun* of a report of the 'teaching swearing' allegation and the demand that the head be 'dismissed', the teacher involved be 'sacked' and the head of department responsible for the Personal Relationships and Community Service course be 'fired': 'A teacher gave his mixed class of 13 year olds a lesson on four letter words . . . The school has wiped out thirteen years of moral upbringing with this orgy of dirty language.' Journalists from the *Mirror*, *Sun* and *Express* came in swarms and were soon interviewing the Parents' Action Group. The headlines read:

School in Swearing [*Daily Mail*].
Parents Cane the Cursing School [*Daily Mirror*].
'Four Letter Lesson' School Scandal [*Sun*].

There was an avalanche of bad news that week. The building felt as if it were under siege. Just going into the building was acknowledged as a gesture of loyalty and resistance. Eleventh session figures significantly increased. Tutor group areas and decorations became more extensive and elaborate. Students worked yet more closely alongside teaching staff than they had done previously. The fifth form—the first fifth form of fully Sutton Centre pupils—all had the same tutors with whom they had begun. They took their seniority very seriously. It was as though everyone in the fifth form had been made a prefect.

The authority had made its feelings plain; Sutton Centre was out of favour and the governing body suspended. The protesting parents represented eleven children out of over 1,500. Four of their number were spokespeople and were corresponding and talking with the press. All had requested that their children be removed from Sutton Centre and go to a more traditional school. The request had been granted and would take effect in the New Year.

The *Notts Free Press* had thought that once the issue was opened it would become a popular cause; it had assumed that a mildly anti-Sutton Centre line was the right one to take. Its post-bag in one week, though, was ninety seven letters in favour and four against. The *Notts Free Press* changed its line into an insistence of not damaging the good work which had been done and insisting upon fair play. Its own contribution to fair play was to print four letters 'against' and four letters 'in favour' under the headline: 'Both Sides of the Row'.

Stewart Wilson spoke to the press too, but only the *Notts Free Press* and the northern edition of the *Nottingham Evening Post* carried his words. So many tensions had been tightened into polar positions: that of the county's Conservative south and the socialist north; Sutton Centre and its amalgamees; Sutton town's respectable and aspiring groups; the teaching profession's division over traditional and progressive methods; Sutton's influential townspeople and the challenge to them from Stewart Wilson, his charisma and his egalitarian philosophy.

Union reaction

The staff unions were the NUT with 54 members and the NAS with 24 members; there were 11 non-union members. The unions had to decide how to respond to the proposed independent enquiry.

On the one hand they were disturbed at the suggestion of having a non-professional body look at the activities of the Sutton Centre staff. On the other hand there was the possibility that an enquiry would help to clear their members of the allegations that had been made against them. But the teachers' unions could not agree on a joint response to the situation. On 2 December, the NAS spokesman was reported as saying that 'the union felt such an enquiry was not essential to the good name of the school and our members'. The NUT response was to oppose an independent project group, and insist that education inspectors conduct the enquiry. As they put it graphically, 'after all, when there's trouble at a pit, it's a mining inspector that's called in'. This point would not be lost on a mining community which had seen an enquiry into the Sutton Colliery disaster of 1955.

The NUT said that they were officially 'in dispute' with the authority until the question of who was to conduct the enquiry was resolved. On 18 December, the county council gave ground and declared that the enquiry would now be made by Her Majesty's Inspectorate, who would start work on 6 February 1978 and hold a full-scale inspection of the school. The council did, however, reserve the right to set up its own enquiry.

The parents' action group

The parents' action group were seriously alarmed at the turn of events. They feared that the successful union pressure on the county council would produce an enquiry that would be a 'whitewash' of the school. One of their members was quoted in the *Mansfield Chronicle Advertiser* as saying, 'If this whole thing is whitewashed then we will set up a stall in the Idlewells Shopping Precinct and let anyone who wants to see the kind of filth that is being taught at that school.' They began circulating a new petition which when complete was said to contain 300 signatures. They sent the petition to Dr Rhodes Boyson, the Tory shadow spokesman on education. He replied to the parents that 'the school should indeed be investigated'. His statement marked a crucial change in line of attack. Dr Boyson did not mention swearing or sex education. In his opinion, 'pupils ought to be able to sit public examinations if their parents wished'.

The PAG members now numbered five—those who had been elected on 25 October. All but one did transfer their children to another school by Christmas.

The parent governors

The response from the three governors was a statement which expressed full support for the head and the staff at the Centre, criticised the parents' action group, and went on to demand that any investigation of the school should include consultations through the parent governors with the governing body. The statement ended by calling for the special project group to be set up on a proper professional and educational basis. Over the weekend the parent and staff governors met at the home of the Centre chaplain to draw up a press statement and write to the area education officer, chief executive and chairman of the board of governors together. They deplored the route taken by the parents' action group in making representation directly to the county council and not through the correct channels of head, governing body, or director of education. They pointed out that the swearing lesson had been exploited by a 'supposedly responsible member of the community', Dr Stein. They wrote that the critics had had an opportunity to make their views public at the Friday meeting of 25 November but had not done so—and on the contrary the 400 parents who had come had expressed full support for the work being done by the school.

The school council put together its own petition of support and collected 1,200 signatures from pupils in three days. This, too, appeared as a letter in the *Notts Free Press*. Every week there were more letters in the *Notts Free Press* and frequent interviews and statements in the *Evening Post*.

Stewart Wilson delivered a strongly worded press statement on 21 December. He asked for the findings of the enquiry to be made public. He said life had been made intolerable for pupils and staff because the school had been subjected to 'trial by the media'.

On the same day, the end-of-term cabaret was, as ever, the barometer of the Centre's climate. There were over three hours of hilarity as if to say 'united we stand and we shall only fall when doubled up with laughter'. Tutor group parties had ranged all over the Centre for a week as students, too, had had their moment of near-frenzied farewell. Staff and students knew there would be changes in the New Year; for each other they showed the strength of support required to survive. The biggest bonus came from a truly simple truth: teachers, parents and pupils just did not feel guilty. There had been intense self- and collective criticism openly expressed for years but that had been to make things better, not because they had been going from bad to worse. In essence there was confidence; when the inspectorate came into the building they would be met by people who had a fair taste of their own success.

On the last day of the year, the recreation manager added his own touch. There had been graffiti on the outside doors of the sports hall during the weeks of distress. The recreation manager, along with the doctor-councillor, felt there should be severe penalties and vigilante patrols.

6

Two trials together:
January to April 1978

January 1978

On the staff's return in January 1978 they were greeted, as a preliminary to the full-scale inspection by the HMIs scheduled for 6 February, by a stunning piece of news. By letter, Stewart Wilson announced that he was resigning as head of the school and taking up a new post at Livingstone in Scotland.

It was so hard for teachers and parents to make sense of this news. Only months beforehand Wilson had been saying that it took a generation to consolidate community education; that with five children of his own there was still at least another ten years of there being a 'Wilson junior' at the school; that he liked the town very much and that he was prepared to stay and see the job through. What, then, changed his mind?

He gave two reasons. The first was that the building had been financed in two stages but it was still not complete, nor was completion in sight. The second was the principle of management. He was incensed at the obstacles to a common commitment which had been systematically placed during the first four years:

It was this frustration — the frustration of seeing the need for one

clear policy for Sutton Centre and the impossibility of ever
achieving it on the present management structure—which finally
persuaded me to accept this new post in Scotland with overall
control of the complex and one parent body. But even then,
leaving a place like Sutton Centre which becomes a way of life is
one hell of a wrench.[1]

Staff were stunned and upset; it was hardly the best preparation for a full-scale enquiry by the HMIs. Privately, and not
without feeling guilty, teachers began to apply for other jobs.
Wilson's decision blew like a strong wind on a dry dandelion
head. There would be the dispersal of staff pursuing their own
careers; and they stood a good chance, having been at a celebrity
school.

The local newspapers had gone quiet now. It was as though,
the trial date having been set, the matter had become *sub judice*.
The national media spoke solemnly on the issues. Their messages
were the same. They spoke in favour of a trial by peers rather than
a trial by ordeal. Their position was that there should be fair and
professional play.

The attention of the national press had been sought by
Nottingham University's resident research officer. He had writ-
ten a cool account of the events to date and sent a copy to them.
New Society printed an edited version.[2] The *New Statesman* sent
freelance reporter Tim Albert; his article, 'How to Damn an
Experiment', spoke of Sutton's situation as:

> a useful lesson on the apparent impossibility of bringing about
> educational change in this country, but also on how political
> dogma coupled with uninformed parental competitiveness can
> wreck painstaking and well meaning education experiments . . . as
> the dust begins to settle on the unimplemented Taylor report,
> whose recommendations would at least ensure that political gam-
> sterism is kept under control by strong boards of governors and
> properly laid down procedures, the future of Sutton Centre is well
> worth thinking about.[3]

The Times Educational Supplement gave an account of events
under the heading 'Showpiece Comprehensive goes on Trial'. Its
editorial said:

> The affair shows how important it is that HMIs should keep, and
> even develop, their inspecting function: it is an immensely diffi-
> cult job to assess educational objectives and standards, and in

circumstances of local controversy one that is often best done by national, not local, experts.

No doubt the attention of the national media had been a further influence upon the county council's decision to allow an HMI inspection. In that sense the school became more evenly matched with the employer. But at the same time the even balance went against the school as it had done when the *Notts Free Press* regularly printed four letters for the school and four letters against it. The protesting parents had removed their children, and so now, at least openly, there were four absentee opponents being evenly balanced against hundreds of supporters. The opposing parents had actually already got almost all of what they wanted. Their children had left and Stewart Wilson was leaving. They waited to be called to testify without anything like the level of concern with which they had begun.

February 1978

The governing body was at last summoned, and the staff governors were promptly asked to leave. The director of education asked the parent governors to accept Mr Tom King as the next headmaster. There would be no search, no advertisement, no interviews and no selection panel for a new head. In the director's opinion it was vital that a new head be appointed, a local man trusted by the authority, ready to take over straight after Easter.

Tom King was truly a local man. He had begun work as a joiner and been recruited to Westbourne by its head, Frank Allen, to teach woodwork. He rose to being deputy head there and then became deputy at Ashfields. Then he was head of Hillocks, another old, small, secondary modern school in Sutton. Next he was head of inner-city Claremont, Nottingham's oldest secondary modern boys' school. He was well connected in many directions. Frank Allen, a leading Rotarian, had been at school with the director of education. Professor Wragg, Dean of Education at Nottingham University, taught one class a week at Claremont School, and Tom King's wife was the sister of Michael Gallagher, the leader of the minority Labour group on the county council. Mr King had been a Sunday school superintendent at a local pentecostal church for nearly twenty years.

The parent governors agonised, hesitated, and were then persuaded. There was no other item on the agenda. They had agreed to approve the appointment of a head whom they had not met or seen.

The National Union of Teachers objected to the absence of due process but on this occasion their objection was wholly ignored. The union was, in the same month, preparing industrial action in support of a pay claim at national level; at local level relations with the employers were rapidly deteriorating. Eighty community teachers in primary schools were also going to be subjected to an inquiry. The library book expenditure had been eliminated entirely for the whole financial year. Teachers' representatives on the council's education committee came in for some menacing scorn. The arbitrary appointment of one headmaster was more a matter of irritating proof than a cause for crusade.

Probably the most important single decision had been taken and taken well in advance of the enquiry and its report. Early in February, too, the enquiry was pre-empted by an education committee decision that all Nottinghamshire schools would make provision for 'O' level examinations. The new head would have new rules to enforce. The appointment of a new man to the 'hot seat' who would 'take control of the school' brought the local press back to the boil. The trial by media would continue on its course of both articulating opposing sides and accelerating the decisions of all those directly involved.

The visitation from the HMIs began on 6 February. An HMI team of seventeen inspectors covering the full range of curriculum activity arrived to spend a week in the school. They stayed at a motel and spent the week talking to teachers about the curriculum, viewing classes at work and determining what should go into their report. The inspectors were not interested in the causes of the enquiry. They said their purpose was to inspect the form and content of teaching; it was a matter of standards.

The inspectors were most enthusiastic over the masses of paperwork available which allowed them to study how the curriculum had developed. The geographer worried that environmental studies failed to make his subject distinctive. The musician was upset by the bubbles in the carpet in the music block floor. Their chairman wanted to know about the catchment area but not about the social class of parents. The 'kids', it was generally agreed, were just 'great'. They were cheerful and cheeky, helpful and happy; they might even have enjoyed having special visitors for a week. The previous term's confidence seemed justified for surely the HMIs could not have found that much to really object to? Stewart Wilson congratulated his staff in the light of a report he had been compiling himself that week. He read out the telegrams and messages of support from schools both far and near. There was a 'camaraderie of the trenches' developing along the front line of progressive education. The next week he told staff that chief inspector thought the report would be available by Easter, but he was not prepared to guarantee that it would be made public.

There was camaraderie in trenches elsewhere too, a camaraderie which could be made public. The Centre enquiry continued to be attracting more points of polarisation. But now the newspapers seemed to be seeking to influence the outcome or insulate opinion holders from it. *Quest*, a religious education guide used by Sutton Centre and other Notts schools, was criticised by members of the West Nottingham Conservative Party for providing 'a communist manifesto for left wing teachers' (*Evening Post*, 21 February 1978). A protest resolution requesting the book to be rescinded was to be put to Mrs Minckley, chairperson of the county education committee, and to the national Conservative Party central council meeting 'in the hope that as a result teachers will be instructed not to use sections of the book'.

The *Notts Free Press* also found opposition during this interim period by featuring a major article, 'Traders Unite to Stop Teenage Shoplifters: Town Shop Ban to Beat Pilfering' (17 February 1978). The stealing was blamed on children below the age of sixteen. The Pricerite assistant manager stated: 'Kids come through the Idlewells Precinct to and from school and it's easy for something to catch their eye.' A branch manager of a shoe shop 'now keeps a monkey wrench in his belt as a deterrent to young offenders who work in small gangs and often try to fight their way out of trouble'. By inference, Sutton Centre was the offending school.

Also while the enquiry reports were being compiled, the *Evening Post* councty council affairs reporter David Levine, considered the implications of the forthcoming reports (2 March 1978). He linked the enquiry with the crisis of choosing between 'progressive' and 'formal' methods of teaching children: 'the results of the enquiry will be a pointer to the way education should go during the next decade'. His hope was that enquiry committee members would choose the method 'which is best for the children, for the teaching profession and . . . for the country itself—sensible and disciplined lessons aimed at giving pupils a sound base for their future working and social lives'. The article went on to say that calling members of staff by their first names erodes respect, that youngsters 'respond to a firm hand', and that the brightest pupils should be encouraged to take the highest level exams. Levine concluded his view of schooling by claiming that 'good comprehensive education is about . . . encouraging the best in a child and helping him, or her, to develop those talents. It is hardly fair, or democratic, to design the system to bring everyone down to the lowest common level.'

The chairman of the county council announced on 25 February that a special project group would soon enquire into allegations that had been made against the school—ten allegations of a non-academic nature. The special project group was an extraordinary body both in composition and constitution. The chairman, Walter Miron, was chairman of the East Midlands Regional Development Council with many further connections, while the other members were all leading figures in their own field. Major Bradshaw was chairman of the Sutton School Governors; Professor Wragg was Dean of Nottingham University's School of Education; Canon Roberts was the educational adviser for the Southwell Diocese and Walter Laughton had previously been chief executive officer of the Sutton Urban District Council.

The enquiry opens

Four parents from the action group were invited to give evidence. Four parents who 'supported the school' were also asked to attend. The teachers' unions were invited to send their lawyers to the hearing. The NAS did so but the NUT boycotted the event. The curious process took place in Sutton Baths lounge on Friday 27 February. The allegations had been listed at the meeting of 21 November at County Hall. They were:

1. Stewart Wilson's daughter was studying an 'A' level at nearby Ashfield Comprehensive—this was favouritism.

2. The head of Westbourne had promised that the fifth year group from Westbourne would be taught by ex-Westbourne staff when amalgamation took place but this promise had not been kept.
3. One school bus and some drivers had no PSV licence.
4. A daughter was beaten up at the Centre on 11 November. This attack had not been adequately dealt with.
5. There had been a repeat of the 'swearing lesson' on 18 November.
6. The head teacher had failed to implement the dismissal of the homosexual caretaker. (He had been dismissed as a result of parent pressure and the promise made by the councillors.)
7. The head had urged pupils to discourage complaining parents from attending school meetings.
8. Children of complaining parents were harassed by staff.
9. The head had called a meeting on 25 November in order to impose his will on parents.
10. The noise and stench of urine running down the walls due to blocked toilets in the maths department had adversely affected the day centre for the handicapped.

The committee settled to their task with gusto. Indeed they laughed and joked all day. In the late afternoon they said quite plainly that they should never have been called, that the allegations should never have been heard or listened to and that they had no substance. The protesting parents were humiliated. Each time they had tried to bring up the question of learing 'about swearing' they had been told that it was not one of the allegations. By the end of the afternoon they realised that most of the laughter had been at their expense. The independent inquiry came and went in a day.

In interview the two key parents' action group members said that this enquiry 'did not treat their allegations seriously'. One particularly resented a question from Mr Miron when he asked whether it was 'noisy urine running down the walls'. The parents' action group felt that the enquiry procedure was daunting; they had to face a clutch of lawyers unprepared. They also felt they had been betrayed by County Hall since they had been informed that no minutes of their meeting of 21 November had been taken, yet they found that minutes were available to the special project group. Finally, they felt again that this enquiry too, like the HMIs' enquiry, had deliberately ducked the issues of the swearing lesson: the chairman had declared that it was not within the enquiry's terms of reference. Professor Wragg performed a remarkable feat for key participants. His phrase that there had been 'a drama without villains' was gratefully received by all, and became banner headlines the following day.

March 1978

The NUT industrial action began. There were to be no working parties and no dinner-time duties. This would mean that at Sutton Centre 1,500 children would be emptied out of the school and into the town. The pupils did not want this to happen and the school council put forward an alternative. School council reps would take responsibility for their own teaching area; that is, tutor groups would discipline themselves. If they were allowed to remain in the building then they would give an undertaking that no harm would come to it. Stewart Wilson and the staff meeting agreed to this.

   Both the building and the town centre no doubt benefited from the arrangement. This agreement came in the midst of turmoil. It meant that the students were carrying the culture onwards; they could innovate in the interest of the school. One brief example of this was their handling of the dinner-time discos, as Colin Fletcher's fieldwork notes show:

   I was walking down from the office and was stopped by two 4th formers. They asked me would I run the disco as the withdrawal of dinner time staff threatened to stop their event. I agreed. I was taken up to the deputy's office and given a roll of tickets and a biscuit tin, and then down to the disco. There were five girls resting against the wall. The main lights went off and the coloured bulbs began to flash. Boys and girls began to stream in through the door. Each paid 2p and was given a ticket by the two boys who had been waiting there when I arrived. I was brought a hamburger so that I did not have to leave my station.

   There must have been 80 or 90 people there. The floor was full of girls dancing and I could make out brief movements in the shadows beyond. The main light flashed. 'Put that fag out Billy,' said the DJ. 'Come on, I can see you.' The beat went on. 'Come on now Billy, there will be no more of this until you do!' It must have been put out.

   The lights flashed again. 'Last one now, what will it be?' there was so much shouting of choices that it was impossible to tell if anybody had actually got their request. The light went on. 'OK, that's it, we'll have to go now.' They slipped away as swiftly as they had come. The roll of tickets and the biscuit tin were put back in my hand. 'Just count the money and put a note on Bob's desk,' he said. 'It's for school funds.' I did, there was more money than the tickets accounted for, they had obviously been more keen to get the money than to give out the tickets. That 2p per person, Tuesday's dinner time disco, raised £1.32. Also present had been one passing adult; inserted like a life-size photograph into the space normally occupied by teachers voluntarily. It was the pupils who reminded us of what was done at Sutton Centre. The pupils carried many distraught teachers along with their expectations of what was normal and usual at school.

Some staff felt the visitation by inspectors had been their finest hour, a tidal wave which carried a host of exciting happenings with it. A pupil was runner-up in a national debating competition. Rugby, athletics and music successes were extraordinary, with teams unbeaten for years or winning contests entered for the first time. But key staff were already leaving; the chaplain and the course director for Communications and Resources were going to be Stewart Wilson's new deputies. The teacher who had held the jewellery sale for school funds was off to sell gold and silver full time.

April 1978

Staff and parents were waiting for the HMIs' report. It had been promised 'as soon as possible'. In the last week of term hopes were raised by rumours that there would be a statement soon. Then, in a telegram press release, Mrs Shirley Williams, the Secretary of State for education, let it be known that while there were some 'justified areas of concern' the inspectors had cleared the school of any charges of bad education. Indeed the inspectors were enthusiastic; they had been impressed by the vitality. Mrs Williams had balanced this enthusiasm against 'concern'.

The 'justified area of concern' was the refusal of the school to do 'O' levels; preventing, that is, pupils from entering public examinations should they or their parents so wish. The county council education committee had passed a resolution that all schools should offer 'O' levels, and Mrs Williams's telegram noted that change was in hand in this respect. The HMI report did not mention swearing. The pressure upon the school had moved away from an 'offending' piece of the curriculum towards insisting that its central purpose be changed. The headmaster would be forced to implement 'O' levels, which could, in turn, dismantle mixed ability groups particularly in the upper years. In any event, the significant changes happened before both enquiries found the school innocent and indeed exemplary. There would be a new headmaster transferred in after Easter, and there would be 'O' levels. The protesters who by now felt that they had been used fell silent; the staff felt that they had been stabbed in the back. The national press reported the press release as a success to be welcomed: a happy ending.

Stewart Wilson's leaving was a happy ending. The sports hall was full as he recalled his five years at Sutton Centre, thanked those with whom he had worked and asked them to join him at the front. Cleaning ladies made their way with bags of weekend shopping; more and more staff and parents joined Wilson at the front. The parade—it was almost a transfer of the audience from one side of the stage to the other—lasted half an hour. Wilson's last words to the pupils were: 'Remember now, be back on 12 April at 8.45 prompt.' The present-giving went on in the afternoon and evening. Stewart Wilson had part of his profile read out to him. Like that evening's cabaret, it must have left him in no doubt that he was held in affection by a band of astute critics, and that at the moment of greatest unity he had said good wishes and good-bye.

7

Two further years:
opposing forces

The headline of the *Notts Free Press* during the new head's first week read: 'No Promises for Sutton Centre'. In the text Tom King explained that he did not promise any changes as yet, but he must have had a list of obvious things to do and he probably had some less obvious things too. It was 'obvious', for example, that 'O' levels would have to be introduced. At the other end of the scale he gave out blue and red biros for marking presences and absences in registers, which suggests that he thought the record-keeping was slack.

   Behind this small decision there was the local small-talk about children wandering around the town when 'they should be at their lessons'. Communications and Resources was the course which regularly despatched pupils into the town to make investigations about its people and their surroundings. The founding course director had left with Stewart Wilson. Tom King refused to advertise for a replacement. He gave no reason for this, the one major decision during his first term, apart from saying that it was a course built around and dependent upon 'one man'. The six course staff, and the staff at large, thought otherwise. He asked all the other course directors whether C. and R. should continue. Remarkably, they said that it should. C. and R. had played a part in the curriculum development in every course. The C. and R.

staff elected to become a collective rather than have one of their
number acting head of department. King was prepared to alter the
curriculum, but there was no tide of staff opinion upon which
such alterations could be carried.

King spoke to staff meetings as head and chairman and staff
spoke back to him both through the chair. He made a
fundamental change without realising it just by assuming that the
head was automatically the giver of agenda, orders and answers.
As the business of the enquiry was not yet over, he took the 'need
for strong leadership' upon himself. The reports were not due to
be received until May.

The reception at Nottinghamshire County Hall of the HMIs'
report, and that of the independent enquiry, went very badly. The
Labour group tabled a motion of censure which retold the story
and said none of it should ever have happened. The
Conservatives walked out of the meeting and installed their next
year's chairman instead. When the matter came up in the
education committee, the leader of the Conservative group
launched an attack on the standards of teaching in general and
the qualities of teachers in particular. He said, according to
page-one banner headline phrasing: 'Teachers have the Morals of
Pigs.' Councillor Bird's opinions in the accompanying article
were quoted as: 'I don't think sex education should be taught in
schools . . . Consequently we've got Tom, Dick and Harry
teaching sex education in schools and some of them have not got
the morals of a pig' (*Evening Post*, 14 April 1978). The union
representative went into an uproar, as did the Labour councillors.
Councillor Bird would not withdraw his remarks and the meeting
abruptly ended.

Neither report was fully discussed or debated by anyone
outside of the governing body. Five HMI inspectors and their
chairman returned to review their findings. They were concerned
that teachers did not have the opportunity to 'replenish their
vision and inspiration'. They had found a contact ratio of 84 per
cent; that is, teachers whilst at school were with pupils for an
average of 84 per cent of the time. This was a full 12 per cent
higher than the HMIs had ever found anywhere before. 'Such
true dedication', said the chairman of the governors.

The HMI report could not be quoted, for fear of comments
being taken out of context. That meant that the report could not
really be used at all. It was like a private detective's dossier on

employees to the board of directors. To the extent to which it said the school was good rather than bad it had scraped some raw nerve-ends at county level. To the extent to which there were 'good' things, they would have to remain or at least still be recognisable to HMIs in the future. What a dilemma for the head, then: praise from educationalists for innovations of great intricacy and complexity; county councillors with egg on their face; townspeople—middle class and merchants, that is—who were not to be antagonised further by 'a school on the streets', parents who had been right behind Stewart Wilson and knew the school's layout and rationale as well as did the staff, upon whom praise had been heaped.

Tom King left most aspects alone that summer—no discussions on uniforms yet, no breaking down of the block timetable yet, nor changes of course titles. As summer approached, the multi-coloured programme of 'suspended weeks' once again unfolded. It did not look as if King would change that at all. The old 'magic' worked just as well as before. Again, over a quarter of students chose to do Maths all week and some fifth formers were up to 'A' level standard already.

King had had a very difficult term. Outside of ex-Westbourne staff he had no teacher allies. Many of his moves had been frustrated by Sutton Centre practices; not least by a staff which believed that they could discuss and argue on everything. Teachers were that much harder upon him because he had chosen to take the job when it was offered. Twelve more staff were going to leave, almost all of whom had made pointed remarks straight at him. One said: 'I just don't want to see this place become bog comprehensive 1839.' The county council and its officials very much left him to it, which also left him very much alone—apart from what he could learn through his connections. His biggest problem was the utter contrast of the present with his past experience. Here was a 'good' school which should not go down. He was going to be forever compared with Stewart Wilson whilst simply not wanting to be a national figure. His predecessor had crossed the market square one day and those in the Centre rushed to the overlooking windows as the word spread quickly through. King did not aspire to oratory or to such popularity, so how could he make changes?

Events over two years tell two stories simultaneously. King 'normalised' the school and the school 'liberalised' him more

than he thought possible. He came to advocate what had at first
made him apprehensive. Outwardly the school changed much less
than might have been expected. Inwardly he looked for weak links
and tried to work on them. He had his friend Professor Wragg give
the staff a talk on 'welcoming change'. The Professor said that the
staff should look for the improvements that the introduction of 'O'
levels would make.

What happened was a pull in two directions with the result that
there was more change in mentality than there was in machinery.
How staff thought changed more than what they did. They, too,
had their dilemmas of changes and constancies. There were new
staff to be recruited who would be confused by an attachment to
history rather than committed to it. There were, above all, the
deputy heads, who could run the school as it was and reason an issue
down to the last ripple of consequence. They knew that Tom King
had inherited the same management relationships on which
Stewart Wilson had despaired and departed. All staff, of course,
were acutely aware of every hint of change. Visitors were too.
Visitors no longer asked, 'What are you doing?' They often came
looking for change, for deterioration and for the evidence which
would dismiss Sutton Centre as just another school. To begin with,
then, what did change? How were some of the high ideals enslaved?

The end of Communications and Resources was a gradual
dismembering. Teachers in the collective left for jobs in
community arts or as self-employed artists. Each had their rows and
arguments with Tom King, on paper and in person. The
headmaster's argument, and incontrovertible it was too, was that
C. and R. occupied sixth-form space and he now had a sixth form
which needed space. He also thought that C. and R. teaching was
'what any good art department would do'.

The sixth form were indeed a problem. First they occupied the
adult lounge next door to the miners' room on the adult education
floor. They brought their stereo set with them. The stereo set was
up against the miners' room wall. The sixth form expected to
occupy their area in the evenings; in effect, to have informal
eleventh sessions of their own. The classes in the miners' room had
responsible tutors. The sixth form quite often did not. There were
complaints about noise. Adults, with the tensions of their precious
time, felt somewhat besieged by young people making sounds of
having all the time in the world. The sixth form moved to the staff
room.

The staff room did not feel like a normal staff room and it looked as if it was hardly used. After four years of doing without, or using the teaching centre or the dining hall, or squashing into departmental offices, the staff no longer needed a staff room (at least not for themselves). All Centre employees were asked to look upon the room as theirs. A few, a very few, actually did. But dinner time was literally an hour long only, and teachers were combining having a meal with being on duty, or with being on duty voluntarily, and travelling from East to West blocks (as Eastbourne and Westbourne were now known). The sixth form had the large and comfortable space virtually to themselves.

Evening usage of the staff room, directly above the recreational management's offices, was less easy to accept. For then the sixth form had a great deal of privacy, if not too much. Moreover, the sixth form still needed a tutor area which would also be their teaching area.

After three C. and R. teaching staff had left, and one transferred out, the remaining staff were told to base themselves at Eastbourne and do most of their teaching there. Two women with low statuses argued against the head's decision and returned in tears. Nevertheless they continued to improve C. and R.'s essential message: poster work, for example, upon the titles 'Can They Forgive?' and 'There Are More Questions Than Answers' showed a maturity of graphic design, quite different from painting by copying books and postcards. The department 'closed' when one teacher left to become a youth worker and the other was transferred to Basic Skills.

The reprographics function for both the school and the community no longer had any teaching support whatsoever. The equipment remained and two young women technicians were still responsible for the issuing, maintenance and usage of a lot of expensive equipment. Reprographics, both photocopying and offset litho, had become big business. 'School work' copying was half or even less of the total volume; indeed only Recreation failed to make use of the facility. Social Services, for example, regularly incurred bills of £80 or more a month. The usage was so great that (even with the less than economic charge made) the wages of the reprographics technicians were virtually covered—making them of little or no cost to the school whatsoever. In addition there was the benefit of being able to print so much material for the school cheaply when the book allowance had been removed and the general allowance had been reduced. Every week, too, there was the *Sutton Centre Bulletin*, now scrutinised by the head first, and still being printed for every tutor group and every section in the Centre. The headmaster's newsletter upon the new notepaper now headed Sutton Centre School was also a regular 1,500 print run. There was a mountain of work going through the print room.

Both technicians—the secretary/course-material-maker/ video-maker/ equipment-issuer, and the woman in the print room—became answerable to the head. There were no teachers or a course director in between. The group of postgraduate students, on an Educational Management postgraduate course at Trent Polytechnic, who studied Communications and Resources commented that there was no maintenance and replacement schedule and that each woman clung to the immediate space around her respective machine to get her meagre job security.

The head had responded to this report by drafting in a teacher with electronics expertise for four sessions a week to make an inventory for renewal and to repair whatever he could. The latter decision produced spectacular success; all kinds of machines were made to work again. When not in use the machines were locked away. They were now issued to teachers only. There was no longer innovation coming from C. and R. C. and R., it may seem, was destroyed, but it did not disappear. It was reduced from an organic entity to a mechanical function, and that part made to work better than it had been. C. and R. was the biggest single change which Tom King made and had most of the hallmarks of its maker.

Another significant change was the creation of Kelvin's group. Kelvin was a Sport and Leisure teacher, tough, firm, cynical and good-natured. Kelvin's group were fifth formers who were 'difficult' and they met up at East block. The creation of this disruptive unit followed another of the county's policies. The county had decided to decrease 'normal expenditure' and increase 'special expenditure'. There were to be two disruptive pupil units and one school for high flyers. One disruptive pupil unit would be in Mansfield. It would take disruptive pupils, the most truculent from each school in the north of the county, and treat them with a determined discipline.

Kelvin's group began in September 1978 and its creation signalled the end of mixed ability tutor groups and CSEs for all in the fifth year. It meant that some fourth-year pupils would actually be keen to get into it. The majority were boys and members of the emergent skinhead, punk and glue-sniffing gangs. The creation of Kelvin's group was unpopular with many teachers who thought that mixed ability tutor groups were a principle which ought never to be violated.

The school was so big that teachers saw little of each other beyond those in their department and through their year-group tutor meetings. Tom King encouraged year-group tutor meetings by making three senior masters the heads of two or more year bands. The effect of this was to make the general staff meeting less important, and staff attendance began to fall and become dependent upon how long staff were prepared to stay. The 'decision' over C. and R. did not find a single speaker in its favour. Furthermore the contrast of this decision with how staff expected matters to be discussed was so strong that it inspired a sharp and sustained reaction. Papers were circulated. The agenda subcommittee scheduled the next staff meeting as a discussion on the staff meeting itself. After six months of proposals referring to cabinets and quorums it was accepted that there would be two staff meetings thereafter. One would be an information meeting at which the head spoke; the other would be a discussion meeting at which serious decisions would be debated. Tom King had claimed more power; the staff had clawed back the right to dissent.

The atmosphere amongst teachers became less consistent. There was dismay among some long-serving members and a welcome for a tighter regime amongst others. Staff left in appreciable numbers as each term ended. The county policy was to recruit only from the ranks of its existing employees for junior positions. There was a wave of local recruitment. For such recruits Sutton Centre was often a rung on their ladder; their commitment was more conditional. Generally speaking they gave greater emphasis to being a good subject teacher than they did to being a good tutor. There were more departmental parents' evenings but the frequency of home visits decreased.

In the summer term of 1979 the deputy head (community) made a survey of the extent of tutors' home visits. Those who had been in post longer were, on average, making more than ten visits a term in their own time and at their own expense. Their replies revealed a learning process too. In their first year, they had 'sold' and 'defended' the Centre. In their second year they had got to know more about the family and felt more able to assess and influence its effects on their tutees. In their third year, they had turned their emphasis towards the references to local and home circumstances which they could make in their own teaching. The survey itself was a prompt for greater attention to be given to home visits. Its results went beyond the effects of moral pressure because they explained to new recruits something of one of the processes in which they were becoming involved.

The other deputy head focused attention upon profiles. These were revised so that it was plain who was writing to whom—teacher to pupil, teacher to parent and so on. This modification countervailed the tendency towards bland and vague remarks. The working party also produced a school leaving report form by which employers could read a summary of the profile of five years of experience. The sixth form were allowed to discontinue profile writing altogether. In effect, where changes were apparently not being made, modifications and improvements were often to be found. False divisions occurred, and there was the re-emergence of the obstacles which Stewart Wilson had been at pains to identify in 1972. These were the divisions to which any large secondary school is prone and which are all the more likely when economic pressure means everyone has to work so much more. The divisions led to the school breaking up into more manageable units, year bands, departments and teaching blocks. They were divisions which weakened the staff collectively and meant that junior positions were at the very bottom of a number of piles. The divisions meant that the effort of each teacher was more and more dependent upon individual will on the one hand and recognition by the head on the other. To put it bluntly, the emergence of divisions favoured piecemeal and technical changes.

Eleventh sessions, for example, continued much as before. There was still no written contract to the effect that teachers worked a ten session week, one of which was in the evening or at the weekend. Nevertheless, new recruits fell into line and county support (the 10 per cent additional staffing allowance) was neither reduced nor withdrawn. Overall, there were more vocational courses and a few twilight (3.30 to 5.30) sessions. The former enabled 'O' levels to be introduced without rearranging mixed ability groups. The latter made the school more continuous than it had been previously. More significant still was the percentage of participating adults, rising from 8 to 16 per cent. In part, this increase came from adults denied LEA classes. In part, too, the idea was attracting more parents and neighbours than it had previously. Mathematics remained as popular as ever whilst elsewhere new topics were pioneered. The attendances in 1979–1980 were close to 20,000 over the year. There were fewer recorded attendances in the library but that was because the new librarian was an enthusiast for study as distinct from 'playing about and chatting'. Thus by 1980, the provision of eleventh sessions had the status of a tradition. Instead of homework, there was voluntary follow-up work which proved to be most popular with the youngest and oldest age groups.

The same could be said of suspended weeks, whose significance was certainly not lost upon the new recruits. The atmosphere in the school—when teachers had chosen to work alone or with each other, and pupils found their choice had thoroughly mixed up tutor groups and ages doing First Aid or Humour and Comedy, etc.—was one of benign ease. The ease also came from so many choices involving being away from the Centre. It was possible for those remaining to see what the school felt like when it was not crowded in every area. Chance conversations often brought the remark that 'It should be like this all the time!'

Centre News continued right until the last day of C. and R. (although now called *Centre Outlook*). The editorial committee spelled out the facts on education cuts in a hard-hitting article for which they made 'no apology'. Not all the editorial committee thought the community newspaper was truly challenging or that it should be given away because advertising had covered its costs. The subsequent debate, though, remained at the level of first principles. For the *Notts Free Press* was beginning to publish articles on the school's successes. The choir was winning competitions virtually everywhere it went. A sixteen-year old student had gained a grade A 'A' level each year since he had been fourteen. There was also the phenomenon of Griff.

Those pupils who had begun at eleven years old at Sutton Centre were showing diversity and competence in equal measure. Griff regarded himself as just one of this wave of pupils which was now crashing on the shores of mature achievement. He came from a respectable working home in Silk Street. He always wore a sports jacket and tie. His acuity in argument was legendary. It seemed as if he was never wrong. 'Ah, but Griff says so' was enough to settle most disputes over appropriate facts of the matter.

Griff won a national debating competiton with a ten-minute speech on political extremism. Tom King arranged for him to give the speech to a full meeting of the county council. The first mention of Sutton Centre at County Hall (in full session) came with Griff's measured defence of democratic liberties. He went for interview to Oxford University colleges to read law. He accepted the first offer. The second college's interviewer wrote to the school to say that they would have gladly taken him and asked if they could be told of any similar candidates.

Other sixth formers were also offered places eagerly by universities and polytechnics. They had found giving an account of the school a great asset at interview. Indeed most had a number of offers to choose from. Eleven of the sixth form chose direct entry to higher education and six chose to defer to go into local businesses.

What, then, had compounded rather than changed was the confidence of the students; they had put their energies into the school's culture rather than into a counter-culture. The school council had struggled for a while and then regained its strength. One example of this in action that came after the head had broached the possibility of uniform—or at least a beginning with the suggested adoption of grey jumpers. The school council responded by 'declaring' two clothing days during the following week: a 'scruffy day' and a 'smart day'. Defaulters would be fined 5p and the proceeds would go the school fund. Scruffy day was a day of horrible appearances, tatty jumpers and torn jeans. Smart day saw teaching areas looking like sets from *The Boyfriend*—pencil skirts and Sunday jackets. Not much money was made for the school fund; nor were 'uniforms' a live issue either.

Tom King, for his part, was feeling more confident of his grasp of affairs, and becoming more committed to the idea of a community school. In the last issue of *Centre News* he wrote:

Learning must be seen as something which goes on throughout life. It must be seen as something that every member of society gets involved in at some level. Desire, easy access and involvement are the key factors . . . Sutton Centre wants community involvement, invites and welcomes it.

Part of the confidence gained came from the knowledge that the last of the really resentful staff were leaving. Those who remained were holding their ground and staying because they had local ties and were not convinced that there were really better schools to go to. The cabaret acts at the end of term had continued to be coded and loaded—almost curses in some cases. The cabaret of July 1979 was particularly heavy in this respect. There was a respite as there was no great wish for 'an end-of-term do like that' for the whole of the following year.

King turned his attention, and that of many staff, to practical matters. He had the county playing fields department attend to the shrubs and surrounds. The pool and waterfall which had worked for only a day before the fountain pump was stolen was filled in and planted. It was a lost golden opportunity and one less headache. He had partitions erected on the adult education floor, which quartered the large space and doubled the teaching area. The adult education floor then had the only corridor in the building but it was much better used by adults and sixth formers. He picked competent teachers who had copper-bottomed references from people he knew. He promoted from within and drew some teachers' careers closer to himself. He expected people to move on to advance themselves and regularly thanked the leavers for all their hard work over the last two years. His approach was practical rather than precious.

Part of the necessity which he saw in this approach lay in the 'new traditionalism'. There was more talk of standards, discipline and employers' needs than there had been for at least a decade. From this viewpoint, Sutton Centre was just another school and the rest of it was somehow across the road or on another site entirely. King's staff had been humiliated and then all but ignored and were now coping with the invasion for which 'O' levels had been the bridgehead. As much as he tried to play a wider role, he was held more acutely accountable for traditional achievements. All else beyond the school was more of an optional extra than ever before. Nevertheless, the school persisted in 'going community' even if community education often meant parent education as a first priority.

A further part of this necessity came from coping with Recreation. Troubles in this quarter regularly sapped energy. By

1980 no children could go into the sports hall at dinner time without being escorted by an adult; one or two leisure attendants prevented them crossing the barrier. Pupils queued with their ice skates hoping to catch a teacher coming back down from the dining hall. 'Take us through,' they asked.

There were high-points as well as steady tensions. The aftermath of the first Motor Show is a good example. The school had the use of the sports hall over a whole weekend. The PTA set up a stall for food and drinks. Over thirty exhibitors from car dealers to puncture-repair-kit sellers positioned themselves in the hall. The centrepiece was a vintage car on loan from the *Mansfield Chronicle and Advertiser* (the '*Chad*'). Thousands of people came although there was so much space that crowds were not a problem. At least £1,000 was raised for the school fund, and by general agreement it was a good trip out.

The recreation manager's memo to the motor show organiser had said that he wanted to clean the sports hall floor after the show in preparation for Monday evening's badminton. The memo specified that the floor should be clear by 1 p.m. But the *Chad*'s vintage car was not moved by its owner until 1.30. At one end of the hall waited a Sports and Leisure class. At the other end waited cleaners and leisure attendants. The recreation manager ordered the pupils off and went to get his memo. The course director went to the headmaster, who said, 'Stand your ground; I'll be down.' The recreation manager put his shorts and tracksuit top on and began hosing towards the waiting badminton class. Faced with a wet and sudsy floor, the class went elsewhere. In the reception area there was a loud argument between the recreation manager and the headmaster over who would be responsible in the event of an accident.

In summary, then, the school was still not unified. Tom King had for three years tried to please employers, staff, parents and his authority. By recognising the interests of each differently, he gradually enabled the school to come in from the cold. Then came the announcement that the lower school block would be completed by autumn 1981. By that time the decline in student numbers would mean the school could give up West block altogether and just use East block as a field centre. Tom King, too, had managed the conflicts and crises of being a community school in a divided centre.

What happened next is a history which brings us to the

present day, and Colin Fletcher's *The Challenge of Community Education* has attempted to continue the account until the summer of 1983. Rather than become involved in retelling the fascinating story we should return to our central purpose: what do the trials of democratic comprehensives tell us about those schools and about 'politics with a small p'? and how can the latter's essentially undemocratic nature be overcome?

Part three

The issues

8

Lessons and implications

To flout public response had proved fatal to Tyndale and we should never forget the lesson learnt in that respect [John Watts].

We can but conclude that school enquiries are brief periods of public spectacle in a longer process of trial and determined suppression. In each case study a head and teaching staff had gone some way towards creating a new kind of secondary school, a democratic comprehensive school. Virtually at the moment when their successes began really to outshine their failures they were stopped from developing any further. A boundary was set for innovation from within schools. These new schools, which had so recently been held up as shining examples, were subjected to a year or more of hostility. In every case the head removed, as did a large number of teachers. The momentum declined and so did the less tangible quality of staff unity.

Michael Duane was seeking at Risinghill to reform an education based on selection and which defined most youngsters as failures because they were incapable of passing public examinations in quantity. He ran into trouble because he pressed for topics taught to include the issues of sex and race. Risinghill was made the subject of continuous visitations by inspectors and finally phased out as part of a reorganisation of secondary education.

R. F. MacKenzie was seeking to transform the whole of Scottish education by the Summerhill example. It was his failure to 'discipline' a boy who had threatened a master, and his invitation to his staff to consider moving if they did not see education as a process of liberation, which provoked a staff report. The report became key evidence when Aberdeen's education committee decided to dismiss him.

Tim McMullen at Countesthorpe sought to prepare pupils for life in the year 2000. There were thefts from the library and criticisms that pupils and staff were taking policy decisions normally considered the prerogative of the head. Under pressure, McMullen resigned on the grounds of ill-health. The HMI inspection took place a year later.

Stewart Wilson sought to establish a community school which would be a working partnership between pupils, parents and teachers: a place where both the school and the community would become resources for each other. He was accused of protecting a teacher who was 'encouraging pupils to swear'. The subsequent inspection at, and hearing about, Sutton Centre cleared both him and the school. But Wilson had decided prior to the inspection to take a job with sole responsibility for a community education centre elsewhere.

The first questions to come to mind could be, why were four men with a known commitment to innovation, who would all introduce mechanisms for 'pupil power', for example, first chosen and then rejected by their education authorities? Why did such a 'risk' and a reversal occur in such a short space of time? The answers must be in the nature of the trials themselves. Each had an event, a *cause célèbre*, which could stick in the public eye like a piece of grit. Each, too, had rumblings of deep issues of principle, conflicts over pedagogy, which had divided the protagonists since the day the school opened.

	Event	*Deeper issues*
Risinghill (1961)	Survey on racialism	Sex education
Summerhill (1968)	Pupil's knife threat	Corporal punishment
Countesthorpe (1973)	Library thefts	Independent learning
Sutton Centre (1977)	Swearing lesson	CSEs for all 16+pupils

If one considers the dates of the trials they seem to be marking the boundaries to development for each of the deeper principles. These schools were amongst the first to publicly stake a claim for their innovations. Their claims were quickly denied by their employers. Other secondary schools might follow their example but do so later, more quietly and in a more piecemeal way.

The beginnings of innovation

Each head proved remarkable by virtue of propounding a challenging philosophy of education. Their aim was to minimise the divisions between pupils and staff and between head and staff by provoking and permitting changes in learning relationships and the content of what is learned. Each argued that how learning takes place is a key constituent of what is learned; that education for democracy is, in part, realised by democratic learning in schools. Each was concerned with the whole pupil as micro-citizen as distinct from miniature employee. Their active opposition to the subordination of the pupil and their teachers to a regime of certification caught them in a duality of justification. First, there are more important things than examinations; secondly, however, when more important things are built into a school's style, examination successes are a natural by-product. Discipline is part of what is learned, they reasoned. They neither separately provided for, nor made prime virtues of, discipline and examination performance.

The four heads were asking the question, Under what conditions can a modern and lasting education take place? Their responses to this question varied because they started from different positions. MacKenzie was certainly the most philosophical and radical in his stance. His pantheistic position (mankind's development is related to understanding our place in nature and therefore takes place best when we are in direct touch with our natural environment) was allied to a political critique of the existing educational system. As he saw it, 'you cannot have an enduring political change unless it is supported by a cultural change, you cannot have cultural change until you set the schools free from their present function of being the indoctrinators of the status quo'. Duane based his philosophy on that of John Dewey and stressed a belief in human nature and a desire to 'remove fear from children in schools'. McMullen talked of education as a voyage of discovery. He, too, asked questions about the nature of authority and declared a belief in reaching decisions by involving pupils and staff in that process. Wilson railed against the barriers put up around teaching and had a vision of social change through community education. They might all be said to be 'democrats of their day'.

Factors in opposition to change

All four men were appointed in the knowledge that they were innovators with track records to prove that they could innovate successfully. How were they chosen and for what reason? In each case, we believe, the key figure was the local education authority director of education.

On the director of education's head sit two of the biggest hats in the educational hierarchy: the responsibility for the day-to-day running of the authority and at the same time, being an appointee of the education committee, the responsibility for drawing up policy papers that reflect its views. There is an adage that the pupils think the school belongs to the teachers, the teachers think the school belongs to the head, the head thinks the school belongs to the governing body, and the governing body thinks that the school belongs to the director of education. The combination of day-to-day overall control and being a politically astute director gives an overriding impression of being the boss —providing the 'members' (the councillors) acquiesce.

Directors of education are able to initiate changes of policy, policies beyond their politicians' own thinking, by encouraging the appointment of heads with 'ideas'. Directors of education sometimes develop strong ideas about education. Mason, in Leicestershire achieved an international reputation in this respect. From the mid-1950s onwards he mastered a strategy for having comprehensive schools accepted in a county permanently run by a Conservative administration.

All four heads had special relationships with their directors of education. They were hand-picked and initially strongly supported by their directors. The directors were fully aware of the principles the heads intended to put into practice. Even Aberdeen's director was still able, at the point when MacKenzie was sacked, to declare that he fully accepted the principles MacKenzie stood for. It was putting them into practice which he acknowledged as a political rather than an educational mistake.

The problem for the directors who appointed innovative heads was how to prevent them upsetting members of their committee. The directors, as 'servants of the committee', were prone to be the first to feel political pressure. This encouraged them to acquire a 'model' approach to educational innovation. A director could support an innovative school as a 'model' for development of other schools in the authority. The power of the authority, on the other hand, was to reject the prototype and so dismantle the director's laboratory. This was certainly the case at Sutton Centre. The director, ignored in the lead-up to the enquiry, was unable to protect an innovative head. In contrast, Mason had effectively educated his Tory council over twenty years about comprehensive and community education and had already used the 'project model' successfully before.

The directors in question certainly encouraged the four heads during their earliest months and years. They approved of such an articulate and caring attitude towards children. They could well have viewed their average schools with mild desperation and hoped that some of their special heads' enthusiasm would be caught and taken up by their neighbouring schools. The directors probably saw 'child-centred learning' as the next change necessary within their large modern comprehensives. They allowed the heads to become openly on the side of the children, to adopt an aggressive and 'partisan' stance; to give authority to children. This partisan stance was further aggravated by the nature of the educational process to which the heads were committed, a process predicated on the importance of the immediacy of experience in learning. The result was a process of change which, when under way, did not allow for a gradual response to it. Parents or staff, administrators or politicians could all feel provoked by the speed with which they were being asked to respond.

There were also objections to the purpose of change as well as its pace. Some saw the issues in absolute moral terms and felt that a head posed a moral threat to themselves (as staff) or to their children (as parents) or their policies (as politicians). They felt threatened from the start. The first objectors were then joined into an infantry by the local press and local politicians.

MacKenzie dissected the 'respectability first, responsibility later' attitude of his Labour-controlled authority in Aberdeen: 'Labour believed in corporal punishment, the fighting services, the traditional educational system and its authoritarian foundation.' In the end when these beliefs were threatened they overcame the commitment to comprehensive education. Indeed, a commitment to comprehensive education was not in any case a commitment to the principles held by the innovating heads.

Whatever the starting point of the accusers, the end result was the same—a conviction that moral outrage was being perpetrated and that 'they' (as parents, staff, inspectors or politicians) had a duty to stop them. The language of debate was therefore accusatory and what was sought was a confession that the head had sinned. Heads were said to:

(a) favour the pupils against the interests of their own staff by siding openly with the former (MacKenzie and Duane);
(b) be undermining the moral authority of parents by encouraging immoral behaviour or anarchistic behaviour on the part of pupils (Wilson and McMullen);
(c) disregard the interests of pupils as prospective employees and of their employers by challenging the examination system (all four);
(d) be attempting to implement notions of their own about the criteria by which pupils should be judged (all four).

The first hints of impending trouble refer to the headmaster not being 'hard enough'. This criticism refers not to the headmaster's relation with pupils, but primarily to the effect of staff he had picked. The reasoning was that:

1. pupils' behaviour was lax;
2. staff were not strict enough;
3. the head did not discipline the teaching staff.

Clearly this criticism was directed at democratic day-to-day decision-making on the one hand, and at the headmaster being loyal to politically aware teaching staff. The criticism was that democracy is a virtue in another setting, but in schools it obstructs the attainment of awards and regulation behaviour. Thus the schools were held in apprehensive attention, but by whom? To whom was the 'event' so important?

Trigger events and protest

It could be that parents with children just beginning or about to complete their education felt the most anxious. Or it could be that some employers resented the cavalier attitude to creaming, streaming and certification which the schools adopted. But a sociological view would not settle there, it would suggest that solid working-class and middle-class parents were increasingly involved in and impressed by the quality of their children's school experience. The substantial support of these respectble middle- and working-class parents was swept aside by ignoring their petitions and correspondence. At Sutton Centre even the governing body was frozen until most of the damage had been done. The many parents who supported these schools were perplexed by, frustrated with and angry about the trials, but they were not anxious over the schools' declared approaches.

Anxiety was more acutely felt by those parents, teachers and politicians whose status was not so secure: by those whose aspirations depended very largely upon the next generation to confirm their position. Furthermore, some parents and employers were sensing an apparent decline in their social status and this redoubled their efforts to secure traditional 'badges of achievement'. Most of the 'trouble' came from the crumbling middle class or the aspiring first-generation white-collar parents.

Their concern was whipped up by the way in which the school was actively attracting attention. They felt that their children were being used as guinea pigs in an experiment in which they had only one chance. They also sensed that attracting media attention had 'political undertones'; that open socialist and liberal support can transform a school into a political football. They had never been personally reconciled to comprehensive education anyway.

These words are the most positively and most frequently used by critics:

competition, order, control, selectivity, streaming, examinations, standards, teacher accountability, inspections, economy, efficiency.

Thus, although not necessarily devoted to these values and standards, the school in question must answer for its activity in these terms; the dice are therefore loaded in favour of the protagonists.[1]

William T. Lowe, in advising English progressive educationalists on what to learn from in America, refers to opponents'
'hodge-podge of motivations'. He suggests scapegoating; a dis-
belief in publicly maintained schools for all; the desire for personal
and collective power; the desire to save money and a wide range of
personal frustrations. Lowe even suggests that an important personal frustration may be that parents or others want the school to
do for their children what they have been unable to do at home;
that is, 'they may be suffering from their failure as parents'. The
hodge-podge of motivations is a highly volatile combination.

Anxiety itself was not enough to inspire an enquiry: there had
to be a feeling that the schools should be stopped. Such is the
significance of the trigger event, the last straw. Events which
actually started the enquiry going stuck in people's memories. The
events themselves were important, because they focused vague
feelings and because of a more deeply held feeling that 'this
wouldn't have happened if . . .'. They were the first available
piece of incontrovertible evidence. The event was the breach in
the wall, the way in.

Evangelical zeal, then, was felt by the detractors as well as by
those committed to the schools. From the moment of the trigger
event itself rational accounts became literally impossible. All
those who spoke took sides. Once arrested by the event, the whole
edifice was steadfastly dismantled for close examination. It
became a 'model' of a different kind, a miniature version of the
educational world, pinned so securely that there was barely any
movement. From then on there was very little chance of the
model spreading its influence by example.

It is crucial to accept that the schools in focus had made some
real mistakes, that some things were going wrong and that they
had handled the 'politics of events' rather badly. But these schools
were all geared to encouraging criticism and making collective
efforts to put things right. They were not tuned to receiving
criticisms which were supposed to stick like barbed arrow heads.
Their processes were intended to correct errors and their attempts
to do so were often interpreted as being a denial.

The weakness of defence

The heads, looking at their activity from the perspective of educational theory, responded to the charges in different ways. Duane saw Risinghill in terms of an authority being fed a hostile view by the inspectorate and by a group of threatened staff. He was prepared to confess to failure, but only to the failure to support his school adequately. When he talked of the problems facing the school in 1964, he spoke of the inadequacies of building and staffing. MacKenzie also spoke of 'failure', but it was the failure to comprehend the nature of the forces ranged against change. He came to see his initial optimism as naive; 'the first object of those in power is to retain power'. Wilson perceived his failure in terms of a politcal betrayal of the school by the education authority, and of the practical difficulties posed by the dual management of the Centre. McMullen resigned from ill-health, and Watt was able to 'confess' to deficiencies he had, himself, identified.

Each head 'confessed' at some point to 'failure'. They meant very different things by that from their critics, who saw them as 'failing to discipline pupils', 'failing to give a clear lead to staff' and 'failing to provide the kind of education' considered appropriate by their education committees. None of them could admit or ever did admit to having failed in the terms their opponents used against them.

All the heads held the belief that an inspection would clear the school and reveal the truth. The particular circumstances in which they found themselves led to different expressions of this belief. Duane wanted an inspection because he and some of his staff and supporting parents thought that it would reverse the Inner London Education Authority decision to close Risinghill. MacKenzie felt that an inspection would have acted as a holding operation, during which time he and his supporting staff would be able to explain themselves more fully. At Countesthorpe, the inspection was welcomed as an opportunity to reaffirm the principles and methods which McMullen had introduced. John Watt and the staff believed that their innovations could be seen to work. At Sutton, Wilson saw the inspection as an opportunity to stop the clamouring of the 'trial by media'. Although the heads were not hostile to an inspection, their staffs were a lot less sanguine. For the teachers, an inspection meant an examination of their professional capabilities. HM Inspectorate judge teachers on the extent to which they have got it 'right'. What is more, the staff of the schools were uncertain about what was being investigated.

This uncertainty was exacerbated by the fact that the inspectorate's document was confidential and could not be publicly quoted. The demands from staff at both Countesthorpe and Sutton for the report to be made public were never met. The uncertainty was well founded, because quotations were used selectively by both opponents and supporters of the schools. Leakages came from both governors and members of the education committee.

The making of a report

The meaning of a report lies in how it is produced rather than what it says. Duane and MacKenzie were right in believing that an inspection would buy time during which they could move a little, and that the report could find in their favour. But neither visit nor report would have solved their problems. The report is just one phenomenon among many. The trial came too soon in their schools' history and the report would have come too late to give any real protection. A report is intended to produce something for everyone. Accusations have been made and the accusers have to be satisfied. Even when the enquiry report vindicated schools, there was always the possibility of justifying the actions of the protestors and instigators. There was 'a case to be answered'. In effect, the very seriousness of the report legitimised the attack.

The report was also a piece of one-way communication. Like traditional school reports, there was no attempt to involve those being investigated in a dialogue. As a one-way communication it therefore also reasserted the authority's own position. The reporting inspector told the staff at Countesthorpe that the inspectorate cannot at one and the same time report and enter into discussion.

The report is carried out by professional educators, the inspectors, who are entitled to have their own politics, act within the boundaries of their masters' views and be independent. As a result, the report gives marks to individual teachers and to each course, and then critically comments upon the school's objectives. Perhaps the report can only be read by those who will seek for comments in support of their own views or actions. A dispassionate reading could well focus upon inconsistencies and points of blatant political influence, and set out to contrast 'recommenda- tions' with what really happened. Is it really conceivable, for example, that reports on MacKenzie and Duane would have recommended their removal from the position of headmaster? Would not the grounds for such an action also apply to a number of other heads?

The report is wracked by the following stresses:

(a) Professionals are called in by politicians.
(b) Professionals judge teaching activity by one set of criteria and purposes by another.
(c) The report 'takes account of' the 'political climate' for its recommendations.
(d) It is outdated by political decisions before it is published. It is redundant to all but historians.

The purpose of an enquiry is not, therefore, to produce a report. At the report stage its function is to have all immediate particip- ants engaged in one set of activities whilst major decisions are being made, or have been made, elsewhere. Having to seek a report, submit to an inspection, await the outcome, read it carefully and accept that it is then out of date is paralleled by a growing awareness of probable deception. The purpose of these enquiries was to leave progressives in no doubt as to their defeat by traditionalists. Enquiries are thus an escalation of *ad hoc* public and political means to produce a specific result: the dispersal of co-operative groupings of innovative heads and teachers. The reports came after decapitation (of the head) and before dispersal (of some or many staff). However, they are not necessarily 100 per cent successful: the two more recent enquiries have neither closed the school nor crushed flat their integrated innovations.

The fate of the parties

The fate of Risinghill was closure. The staff, divided amongst themselves over Duane's methods and goals, were re-allocated within the ILEA. The pupils, despite protests, were also relocated. Those parents who joined Duane in clamouring for an enquiry into the decision to close Risinghill were ignored. Duane himself was made a peripatetic lecturer and was to tour institutes of higher education discussing the needs of a truly comprehensive system.

Summerhill, after MacKenzie was sacked, was temporarily run by a deputy director. The school settled quickly, without implementing the series of changes demanded of MacKenzie, into the 'safe' institution it had been before he came. The tawse returned. Pupils settled to the serious business of passing exams. MacKenzie himself was entirely freed both to develop his theories on the importance of the outdoor environment to learning and to reflect on the nature of the educational experiment he had attempted to create in Summerhill. As he put it: 'Education is either liberation or domestication. And that is what the row at Summerhill was about.'

Countesthorpe survived. Not only did it survive, but the experience strengthened the school in both its convictions and its methods of progressive education. The new headmaster, John Watts, built on the foundations which McMullen had laid. On the cover of the book he edited, *The Countesthorpe Experience*, it is said that the school 'weathered its storms to be hailed nationally and internationally as a lighthouse of innovation, particularly in the fields of staff—student relationships, independent learning, participatory government and community involvement. More than one prominent educationalist has likened its formative effect on maintained schools to that of Arnold's Rugby on the public schools of the 19th century.' The commitment of the governing body and the enthusiasm of a large section of parents and pupils reinforced a staff that was able to survive and to retain its innovations.

Sutton lost a dynamic leader and the seventeen staff who followed his example, but the school was not closed and it continued with most of the practices which Wilson and his staff had first designed. The authority's ruling that 'O' levels be taken was slowly applied. The new head abolished the controversial Communications and Resources department and showed an interest in school uniforms. Staff meetings separated into discussion meetings and information meetings. In time, we suggested in Chapter 8, the new head was largely won over by the school's style. At the same time he also had to contend with falling rolls, financial cuts and the rise of a new traditionalism'—the 'new right' in education. His prime task probably changed from that of development to that of defence in which he, himself, was included.

The base common factor of the case studies was simply the removal of the head. John Watts described Countesthorpe's parents' action group as: 'a passing coalition of malcontents given inflated importance for political reasons'. But Mr Shedd of Sutton's parents' action group thought they had won a real victory. As he put it: 'the standard bearer has gone and the battalions have gone with him'. As we had guessed in Chapter 1, each head suffered the trauma of a 'denigration ceremony'.

The fates of the schools, however, range from disappearance in the case of Risinghill, a reversion to the norm at Summerhill, compromise at Sutton Centre, to the careful maintenance of innovations at Countesthorpe. The short-term consequences suggest considerable contrasts, while the longer-term consequences suggest rejecting the notion of fate altogether. For if the school is not closed then the pupils and staff will pick up the pieces of their shared culture and will continue to receive extensive parental support. Newly recruited staff, those who come after the public spectacle, will probably be attracted to the school's style and atmosphere – by trying to 'fit in' they will be bringing fresh energy to the collective effort.

So, too, the authority may have egg on its face. It may be reluctant to take further action for fear of being accused of victimisation and political malevolence. If the school stays open its culture can continue to develop and it can continue to attract like-minded parents and staff. Furthermore, the authority may think it prudent to 'leave the school alone'. The enormous effort made to survive the trial can succeed in preventing the school's destruction. The point is that the contest is so unequal and the ordeal so costly.

'Politics with a small p'

The case studies are critical incidents which expose the political tensions that every school is constrained by and can contribute to. The case studies also suggest links between everyday politics and major political movements. At the very least political features suggestive of wider political issues and conflicts may be identified:

- Opposition to the head from 'a passing coalition of malcontents' – of staff (Duane and MacKenzie); of parents (McMullen and Wilson).

- An authority's inspectorate in disagreement with the school (Risinghill and Countesthorpe).
- High-status local people against 'modern education' (Summerhill, Countesthorpe and Sutton).
- Politicians who can neutralise the director of education and pursue a policy of attrition to the end (all four).
- Media which will both bias and keep the balance of forces in tension so that the trigger event, main personalities and inevitability of a show trial are the main news items (all four).

Against this formidable array of political constraints is the strength and unity of purpose shared by the head, staff, teachers' unions, governing body, parents and pupils. The more divided these groups are—within and between themselves—the less chance there is of altering the trial process. It is plain, too, that the heads 'failed' to stay out of the local press. When they thought they were communicating with the host community they were antagonising its more discreet influentials. It would have been less provocative to debate their ideas in the specialist educational press, although it would also have been inconsistent with their beliefs. Their 'high profile' is unlikely to have caused their trials; rather it was symptomatic of being an independent local figure, of using the status of their positions to full advantage: that is, of not being factory fodder themselves. If the heads thought that the local media which they used would not just as easily abuse them, then they were naive.

Whilst the four case studies do not prove what social and political conditions produce trials, they suggest the significance of two related kinds of politics, one in the 1960s and the other in the 1970s. Risinghill and Summerhill were brought to trial by Labour authorities. In retrospect these were right-wing Labour authorities then firmly in power and yet at the furthest extent of their distance from the working class that postwar history would deem possible. Countesthorpe and Sutton were brought to trial after local government reorganisation and by a new breed of Conservatives who were small business people in the main and who often had not held political office before. 'Politics with a small p' probably lead to school trials of the kind we have described when the politicians immediately responsible for education have no effective opposition and openly share the values of those against comprehensive schools.

9

Towards the development of democratic comprehensives

How do we go about the defence of political gains? How do we use our experience in order to plan our next advance on the citadels of educational privilege? [MacKenzie 1977: 34]

At the beginning of the previous chapter we claimed that the schools in question were put on trial for being, or becoming, democratic comprehensive schools. What does this term, 'democratic comprehensive', mean as far as the participants are concerned?

Pupils

There are likely to be elections within teaching groups and a congregation of those elected. The latter assembly is often called a school council. Power is held by pupils to elect their spokespeople. Their representatives have the right to meet within school time and discuss matters which affect the school. For example, representatives will not be expected to take existing standards of dress and behaviour for granted. They will also give voice to complaints and proposals. There is involvement in democratic forms amongst the pupils themselves, from which representatives can be elected for an overall council or governing body.

Teachers

The teacher in a democratic comprehensive is likely to be regarded as a member of a course team. There is parity between course teams too, which can be explicit when all those in charge of courses are on the same salary scale. Personal territory may not be closely defined. A whole area of the school may be seen as being held in common with other teachers on the course and the children themselves.

The teachers' staff meeting may have been developed to include the following principles: an agenda subcommittee with representatives from each course which agrees the items for discussion; a rotating chairmanship, which may or may not include the head; and the principle of voting after discussions have taken place. The staff meeting is not likely to be the only meeting in which teachers engage. Instead there are likely to be almost as many working parties as there are issues—on difficult children, curriculum development, relations with parents and so on. Key working parties would probably gel around the uses of the school fund and the opportunity to particiapte in the short-listing, interviewing and selection of new staff.

The head

Hierarchies are modelled on the armed services. In schools the head is like a field general responsible to the chiefs of staff. Quite simply, the head is responsible for everything and therefore technically has power over everything. There is no great or small decision to which he or she cannot append their name. Like the captain of a ship, the Head is 'a captain under God'.

The head's position involves elements of all of the three kinds of authority described by Max Weber. There is charisma or 'personality'. There is the authority of the bureaucrat, as receiver and issuer of all memoranda. There is the authority of a monarch; to reward or punish subjects, do no apparent work and be the sole maker of decisions.

Each of the three kinds of authority is distinctly used by the head in a democratic comprehensive. Charisma is expressed to give staff confidence in their own ability, the abilities of the pupils and the human relationships being developed. The gift is to convince participants that they are members rather than parts, that 'we are all in this together'. Bureaucratic authority is dealt with rather than developed. The flow of meaningless information is reduced to a minimum; a low level of paperwork is expected, and that paperwork which is important is dealt with as democratically as possible by full circulation. The time when the head may be a monarch is in the arena of external relations, as defender and advocate of development. Then the head is rather a lonely and vulnerable figure. It is this latter effort which encourages staff to support the head. Thus a democratic head exerts influence rather than power, an influence which asks for staff support as distinct from compliance.

Parents

In the democratic comprehensive the stress is upon the parent as a co-partner in the process of educating the child. This may be translated as a stand against the conventional forms of parent contact in favour of involvement. The activities encouraged include home—school liaison, open evenings for different subjects and different years of pupil, and open access to the school for parents at most, if not all, of the time. The open access may be more broadly expressed still, with the school being seen as public property and the parents having an immediate and present need as well as right. Open access leads to the development of parent education and parent helpers.

By parent education we mean that parents and other adults can attend classes alongside children and that the feedback from the school is seen as supporting the parents' own role. By parent helpers we mean the availability of numerous voluntary roles, some of which involve helping directly in classes, others of which involve ancillary work. Parents are understood to be people who have educational needs which the school might meet and who have skills which would further educational content for the benefit of all. The logical conclusion of these ideas on parent involvement is the political and practical desirability of there being parent governors.

Governing body

In theory, by virtue of provision in the Education Act 1944, the head is directly responsible to his board of governors, the meetings of which he/she attends as a non-voting member, and is responsible for day-to-day matters via the area education officer to the director of education. In the democratic comprehensive, all sections, or interested parties, have their own elected representatives and there is a balance of interests such that no group holds an effective majority.

Each participant is being asked to share the role of at least one other participating group; parents closer to teachers, pupils closer to both, head closer to staff, governors closer to the head. The belief is that movement towards shared roles creates a more viable institution. It is an attitude based upon the potential for participation, as distinct from emphasising the problems which one group can create for another. The most important single proposition is that the democratic school brings together a re-definition of the roles of all its participants in the hope of greater identification and trust from one to another.

The democratic comprehensive is more than a matter of committed ideals and idealists on committees. First and foremost it is recognisable through the democracy of everyday life, through curriculum choices for staff and pupils, through first-name terms, through comfortable dress and through the messages on its walls and windows. The presence of choices within the areas of curriculum and appearance or dress and the ease of social relationships are all aspects of what we earlier called democracy in learning. When innovations occur in these directions democratic issues can be expected within the curriculum choices too. Here we can not something of an historical progression in our case studies. In contemporary terms Risinghill's learning content included multi-cultural studies; environmental studies had prominence at Summerhill; citizenship, personal relationships and political studies all featured at Countesthorpe and Sutton Centre. A further aspect of the schools' comprehensiveness was to explore

the tension points and possibilities within the continued development of a democratic society. With hindsight we can say that
issues of race and gender, for example, were foci of learning almost
as soon as they became recognised as urgent problems in adult life.
Since pupils were tackling issues which adults were then facing,
they could be said to be being prepared for adult life; they were
becoming 'critical spirits'.[1]

How important such matters are is open to dispute. We are
really directing attention towards evidence that for pupils,
teachers, head, parents and governing body it is their shared,
socially aware school. Our accounts strongly suggest that all four
schools were striving to be or become democratic comprehensives. If this is so then we would expect aspects of self-evaluation
to be present too.

Self-evaluation

All four schools were in new or nearly new buildings. Risinghill
was ramshackled and Countesthorpe and Sutton had the look of a
building site. How important was this extra burden? Summerhill
and Risinghill had strongly divided staff, whereas Countesthorpe's and Sutton Centre's staff were overwhelmingly united. What
difference did staff solidarity make?

Whilst we can raise these questions we cannot adequately
answer them. They stand at either end of a continuum from
practical affairs to professional matters and they were questions
for the participants to put to each other. Unless there was
self-inspection (now called evaluation) there was no preparedness
for an inspection by the authority's inspectors of HMI. Nor would
there be a detailed response to real deficiencies, and many
problems would remain untouched.

As Caroline Benn puts it:

> Every school should also have a way of satisfying itself that what it
> teaches, and how, reaches standards of acceptability that it can lay
> down to be observed, and regularly reviewed . . . criticism can be
> matched against these standards. If it has substance, corrective
> action can be taken — by the school. If it does not then reply can be
> made and the school defended.[2]

this is not to say that self-evaluation makes problems go away.

It does not. Rather self-evaluation takes it for granted that there are perennial problems and asks, Honestly, how well or badly are we coping at the moment? What should we aim for now? The recurring problems include:

- the conflicts between staff and staff groups;
- the rebellious and revolting amongst the pupils;
- the poor relationships with parents and community(ies).

If a collective and democratic approach to issues is not taken then far too much is said to depend upon 'teacher identity'. Problems are individualised and once problems are invested in specific individuals no one profits. Furthermore, teachers are then likely to adopt a polarised view of their own work. Then criticism from the left convinces some teachers that the best description of their job is as an 'agent of social control' and that they should really subscribe to the deschooling ideas of Ivan Illich. At the same time others are susceptible to criticism from the right involving claims that comprehensive schools compel mediocracy and rash experimentation, and fail to achieve even 'minimal standards'.

The point of self-evaluation is to get hold of the contradiction between professional autonomy and political accountability by recognising the rights of different constituencies and openly debating their needs. We would recommend self-evaluation as the only way a school can be sure of its constituencies' genuine support in times of struggle.

This is not the place to spell out details of different styles of self-evaluation; it is an approach which a few teachers have been very busily developing in recent years. The point is that for years to come even 'routine' inspections are likely to reinforce the instability of the comprehensive system and destabilise democratic comprehensive schools.

One indication of the trend is that HMI reports now being published are beginning to show their preference for hierarchical orderliness:

> Time was when they did what their titles would seem to imply — inspect schools. They would swarm over the school for a week, terrify teachers out of existence and then pen a gentle, coded report which, after discussion with a few senior teachers and governors, would gather dust. [3]

Yet, as Delves and Watts wrote:

> There are no regulations that add up to a prescription of how a
> school should be run, and in our changing times, there is no
> certainty that a team of Her Majesty's Inspectors have got all the
> answers for the teachers. Sometimes things will have moved on to
> a point where HMIs have not even got the questions.
>
> Many HMIs have acknowledged a change in role from that of
> judge and jury to one of counsellor, guide and friend. Many must
> prefer to sit down with the teachers and jointly tease out a problem
> together. Unfortunately, their own machinery for inspection and
> report has not undergone comparable redesigning. What schools
> desperately need is help in the techniques of self-evaluation and
> consultation, a totally different mode of giving account of
> themselves.[4]

Her Majesty's Inspectorate, though, has not moved towards
aiding self-evaluation. It is still a step that schools must take for
themselves.

HMI inspectors do remain, nevertheless, a partial defence
even if they are not a party to the development of democratic
comprehensives. They will be called in too late, they will accommodate themselves within the dominant political preferences and
they will pay scant attention to the aims of democratic comprehensives. It is still, however, probably better to be judged by
national experts than by local amateurs. A *Times Educational
Supplement* editorial put this view forward with some strength at
the time of Sutton Centre's enquiry:

> Of course laymen have a right to enquire into the workings of
> schools: no one in his senses would deny that schools must be
> 'accountable' to the public in various ways. But there is a well-
> established form of enquiry, accepted by professionals, and only
> when that procedure has been proved to be unsatisfactory in a
> specific case should there even be discussion of other expedients.[5]

Self-evaluation is a continuous process of preparedness, and
HMI inspections are moments of equivocal professional solidarity. Both are really defensive strategies.[6] In the development
and monitoring of school performance it is likely that pressing
problems like the new arrivals at Sutton or the library book
disappearances at Countesthorpe would be quickly recognised.
Such steps away from the brink would also be more firmly placed if
two other lessons from Sutton and Countesthorpe were taken to

heart. The first is the vital support which came from the vast majority of parents (and others) who had already become involved in the schools' curriculum and everyday life. Both schools' protest groups remained very small indeed and rather than gaining membership and momentum became quite obviously more marginal. Sutton's parents' action group also qualified its criticisms with compliments—even they had had sufficient direct contact to refrain from unbridled hostility. The parents' action groups felt that they had been made into pawns at some point too. They had been held up by the media as prime movers and then had very little say in the subsequent actions.

The media, especially local press, need to be carefully and politically handled by would-be educational reformers. Local press 'barons' are part of the regional aristocracy which is, as we said earlier, apparently easily offended by heads independent of their connections and convictions. Terry Ellis of William Tyndale had only half-grasped this possibility when he acidly remarked: 'Schools that create adverse publicity are bad and receive bad inspection reports: those that "don't make waves" wallow on.'[7] Terry Ellis seems to have made the same mistakes as Michael Duane and Robert MacKenzie. They all came over as people who were high on rhetoric and low on political skills. Their very preparedness to return again and alone to disputes in the local media made them appear figures of a 'left paternalism' even if this impression of their intentions is utterly untrue and unfair.

Political skills ask for an honest and unneurotic relationship with the core groups of 'politics with a small p' which need to be with and in support of the school, as well as a cautious exchange with the peripheral groups who will mount wave after wave of invasion once they have a trigger event to latch on to. Political skills thus chart a middle way between passivity and high-profile innovation, between anonymity and annoying announcements. But if democratic comprehensives are to gain more space in which to develop they also require the existence of a legal process which they themselves can use if need be. Political skills may be sufficient in some situations and yet simply inadequate in others.

Enquiries and due legal process

In our investigation of enquiries we became aware of how

widespread techniques of destabilisation really are. The four cases we studied were the tip of a substantial iceberg. There are constant local authority pressures applied on a smaller and more local scale but serving the same ends. Whilst the different enquiries were taking place, large numbers of schools and individuals made contact to offer sympathy and tell their own stories. Some local enquiries had led to the head of a school losing control over the power to select new staff. Heads spoke of a fear of favouring a candidate openly and resorting to a sign language of encouragement. Others had their budgets reduced. Some had advisers permanently stationed on the premises.

Our study concentrated on the celebrities rather than on the minor actors in what appears to be a day-by-day drama. Those at Sutton Centre, for example, barely realised how much they had in common with other schools, either locally or nationally, until the latter made determined, if dejected, contact. Most recently there was the full-blown drama at Madeley Court School, Telford, in which Shropshire politicians were determined to rid themselves of a head and disengage the school from its community. Once again, the machinations were explained in retrospect in terms of inspections and enquiries.

What is it to be threatened by an enquiry? The circumstances vary from being called backwards and forwards to County Hall to spending months in a courtroom. If mutterings are heard to the effect that there ought to be an enquiry, that someone ought to look into what is really happening, then what should properly take place? Enquiries by body blow or by niggle do not continue indefinitely. Often in the face of denigration and in the full knowledge of impending trauma, the head capitulates; he removes and allows the authority to put in their own nominee. If this is true, then to whom can the schools and their heads appeal?

We have reached the need for another brick in the wall of legal defences for the nation's citizens and social groups. Whereas common law rights apply to individuals (they can sue if they are slandered and prefer charges if they think themselves robbed), institutions such as schools are not entitled to initiate their own defence. When under attack they must endure whatever happens, for however long it takes. For the benefit of all concerned there should be a proper legal process of enquiry. Procedures should be laid down which specify how charges can be brought, how evidence is to be given and taken, how a school or authority can organise its own prosecution or defence and the press access for all participants. The time has come to be absolutely clear about the role of HMI in this respect. They should collect evidence on behalf of an enquiry which is then made public, and be entitled to draw up a separate list of recommendations. Pupils, parents, teachers and the authority should all be represented, entitled to bring charges and counter-charges and produce evidence and submissions.

Guidance should be given on how to organise evidence. So far, it would seem, investigations can only take a school's scholastic achievements as evidence. Clearly such achievements may not be the only goals and so the terms of reference must be broadened. Is the behaviour of children inside and outside school in terms of delinquency, truancy and vandalism merely incidental and actually 'nothing to do with the school'? If staff are absent with obscure complaints for weeks at a time, what does it say about their willingness to go to work? Should this kind of evidence be used? There are few direct ways of measuring a happy atmosphere other than the extent of voluntary commitment and the extent to which 'normal' pathology is missing.

If enquiries were a full legal process and if the kind of evidence we have touched upon was brought into the open, then the judgements reached might be of some use. The William Tyndale enquiry was put together in such a way that the charges could be heard, evidence assessed, and the witnesses cross-examined. Its terms of reference left much to be desired, but at least there was a thorough attempt to assess the credibility of the evidence.[8] Without such safeguards an enquiry, regardless of true guilt, 'brings a sinner to his knees' (R. F. MacKenzie).

We accept Benn's two clear warnings upon elaborate legal procedures; they are a problem in themselves and the very people who are likely to be affected are highly sceptical of their value. As she put it:

> Those who hold investigations, often for the best of mixed motives, find they are never the easy way out they had hoped. In fact they always involve a quicksand of decisions: on procedures, terms of references, balance of membership, criteria for reporting back and, of course, that great two-edged sword: definitions . . .
>
> Often it is those who are the politically committed who find it all the most time wasting, who suspect that much of the labour in fashioning elaborate constructs to protect 'academic standards' or

provide for 'independent assessment' is only camouflage for what is really going on: in effect, the most genteel of political trial.[9]

However, let us not be too parochial or too readily dismissive of the rule of law. By now, in the late twentieth century, we have become used to the idea of public hearings. When motorways are planned, or valleys could disappear under water, or green fields are to be covered over with the tarmac of factories, we hold enquiries. In fact, enquiries have become a regular response to plans for a large and imminent change. Attention has to be paid to the publicly available results of an enquiry. Equally, allegations have to be expressed as alternative strategies before an enquiry can be set up.[10] Considering the parallels, therefore, all large, planned changes in education should be discussed and assessed regardless of whoever wishes to see them happen. The authority should have the right to ask for an enquiry in a school; the school, its head and teachers, should have the right to ask for an enquiry into changes planned for it. Like all defences against bullying or blundering a full legal process is a time-consuming necessity.

Notes

Introduction

1. Colin Fletcher (1978 A); the full text appeared later in Colin Fletcher (1978 B).
2. Virginia Makins (1978: 3).
3. A fuller context for this observation is: 'The movement of population to the suburbs, the closing down of traditional occupations in the inner urban zones, the pattern of post-war redevelopment and reh-ousing, above all the penetration of these areas by speculative development and the private property market have seriously disrupted the organic life and 'natural economy' of the urban working class neighbourhood. This process has also left the urban school visibly stranded—beached—above the retreating social landscape—Stuart Hall (1977: 14).
4. Mike Minchin (1975).
5. See Harold Garfinkel (1967: 57–60) for an experiment on the determinants involved.
6. George Taylor and John Saunders (1976: 163).
7. One account of which is: 'A recent Inner London Education Authority survey showed that inspectors spend only 5% of their time in schools. In practice, before the Tyndale affair, inspectors were rarely seen in the classrooms. Their role, as far as schools were concerned, was two-fold: firstly a benign one, working as advisers, mainly to head teachers; secondly as "trouble-shooters", moving in on potentially difficult situations to protect the authority's image" — Ellis (1976: 113).
8. Virginia Makins (1975; 1976: 8).
9. Virginia Makins (1975; 1976: 8).
10. Stuart Hall *et al.* (1978).
11. Terry Ellis *et al.* (1976: 117, 118, 123, 125 and 149).

12. John Watts (1980 A: 89).
13. John Watts op. cit.
14. Barry MacDonald (1976: 131).
15. John Watts op. cit.
16. Roger Dale (1979: 96).
17. David Reynolds and Michael Sullivan (1980: 121).
18. David Reynolds and Michael Sullivan (1980: 124).
19. David Hargreaves (1982).
20. David Hargreaves (1982: Preface).
21. Harry Rée, the editor of the Community Education Development Centre's newspaper, *Network*, edited the county council's report and appended his comments where appropriate. The same issue included a long one-page article on its 'Reverberations' (Vol. 3, No. 10, November 1983). These excerpts are taken from Rée's report and include his emphasis.

Chapter 1

1. Inspectors' report to the governors' meeting, Howe Dell School, 1950 – quoted in Berg (1968: 35).
2. Later to become Sir John Newsom and chairman of the Central Advisory Council for Education – quoted in Berg (1968: 26).
3. Ibid.
4. Tenen – quoted in Berg (1968: 29).
5. Berg (1968: 32).
6. Berg (1968: 35).
7. Berg (1968: 44).
8. Berg (1968: 62).
9. Berg (1968: 49).
10. Berg (1968: 111).
11. Duane, in correspondence with the authors.
12. Berg (1968: 148).
13. Berg (1968: 115–16).
14. Berg (1968: 125).
15. Berg (1968: 132).
16. Berg (1968: 111).
17. Berg (1968: 171).
18. Berg, in correspondence with the authors.

Chapter 2

1. R. F. MacKenzie (1970: 134).
2. Willem van der Eyken and Barry Turner (1969: 124–44).

3. R. F. MacKenzie (1977: 6).
4. 'It was true that many teachers rarely used the belt; but for others this punishment remained a regular part of class routine' – R. F. MacKenzie (1970: 119). Chapter 6 of *State School* is titled 'The Belt' and deals with an experimental period at Braehead School which ended when 'the teachers had got together and sent a statement to the Director of Education saying that my refusal to allow them to use the belt had made it impossible for them to do their work and asking for his advice. I think the statement was signed by every full-time certificated member of the staff' (1970: 124).
5. R. F. MacKenzie (1977: 22).
6. R. F. MacKenzie (1977: 32).
7. R. F. MacKenzie (1977: 34).
8. R. F. MacKenzie (1977: 33).
9. R. F. MacKenzie (1977: 35).
10. R. F. MacKenzie (1977: 37).
11. R. F. MacKenzie (1977: 38).
12. R. F. MacKenzie (1977: 23).
13. R. F. MacKenzie (1977: 20).
14. R. F. MacKenzie (1977: 20).
15. R. F. MacKenzie (1977: 58).
16. R. F. MacKenzie (1977: 82).
17. R. F. MacKenzie (1977: 83).
18. R. F. MacKenzie (1977: 83).
19. R. F. MacKenzie (1977: 93).
20. R. F. MacKenzie (1977: 95).
21. R. F. MacKenzie (1977: 102): 'The exchange of letters was like a game of chess played with my son when we have reached the stage at which it is only a question of how long it is going to take him to box me up completely. The Director's bishops and castles and pawns were closing in.'
22. R. F. MacKenzie (1977: 105–6).
23. R. F. MacKenzie (1977: 108): 'A comparison of a randomly chosen week in 1971 and 1972 with the same week in 1975 showed a considerable decrease in '75 as far as the pupils in the first three years were concerned.'
24. R. F. MacKenzie (1977: 27).

Chapter 3

1. Tim McMullen quoted in Gerald Birnbaum (1975: 351).
2. Tim McMullen (1968: 65).
3. Tim McMullen (1968: 67).
4. Tim McMullen (1968: 64).

5. Tim McMullen (1974).
6. Stewart Mason, quoted in Birnbaum (1975: 347.
7. 'The building seems lavishly equipped, but only because they have spent money on carpets instead of walls, and on an offset litho machine and three video recorders instead of a swimming pool and sets of text books: "We've spent slightly over the odds for a new school, perhaps two or three thousand pounds", said Mr McMullen'—Makins (1975; 1976: 4).
8. Stewart Mason, quoted in Birnbaum (1975: 348—9).
9. Birnbaum (1975: 366—7).
10. Editorial, *The Times Educational Supplement*, 4 September 1970.
11. Ibid.
12. During just the first six months of the school twenty one reports were filed in the local press, the *Leicester Mercury*. See Open University (1976, Item 1: 16).
13. Virginia Makins, in Open University (1976, Item 1: 5).
14. Birnbaum (1975: 355).
15. Birnbaum (1975: 354).
16. Virginia Makins, in Open University (1976, Item 1: 6).
17. Tim McMullen (1972).
18. Open University (1976, Item 1: 16).
19. 'Mason never understood Tim's commitment to staff democracy. He assumed that, like himself, Tim was only interested in democracy as a more effective and humane as well as a more up-to-date method of securing the goals he had himself determined on. This emerged with startling candour, in a series of letters exchanged between Mason and Tim on the subject of Marion McMullen's appointment to the staff'—Michael Armstrong, quoted in Open University (1976, Item 2: 27).
20. John Watts, in Open University (1976, Item 2: 11).
21. John Watts, in Open University (1976, Item 2: 7).
22. John Watts in a personal communication with the authors.
23. Tim McMullen (1974).
24. Ibid.: 13 and 15.
25. John Watts (1980).

Chapter 4

1. Stewart Wilson (1980 A).
2. Stewart Wilson (1980 B: 120).
3. Stewart Wilson (1980 A).
4. Stewart Wilson (1980 B: 121—2).
5. Stewart Wilson (1980 A).

6. Colin Fletcher (1980 B: 2−3).
7. Colin Fletcher (1978 B: 52).
8. Taken from the Communications and Resources profile card.
9. *Sutton Centre News*: winter 1975.
10. James Stone (1975).
11. An average of 182 free meals per day were taken during the year.
12. Barry Elsey and Ken Thomas (1977).
13. The 'equal status' given to the recreation manager derives from a feasibility study recommendation: 'We suggest that, parallel with the Head, and of equal status with him should be a Manager of the recreation facilities, responsible for provision for the youth service, the activities of voluntary organisations, the sports centre, town functions and young children. He would also be the liaison officer with the social service elements and the Probation and Careers Advisory Service'. By 1977, however, youth provision was separate from both district council and education and the province of Nottinghamshire County Council's leisure services.
14. Stewart Wilson (1980 B: 128−9).

Chapter 5

1. The weekly *Notts Free Press*, established in 1858 as a Whig paper, has a circulation of 19,000 which gives virtual blanket coverage of Sutton (population 48,000) and its surrounding villages. Its offices are based in Sutton, a matter of three minutes' walk away from Sutton Centre itself. Upon the death of its editor in 1967, the paper was bought by T. Bailey Forman Ltd, part of the Nottinghamshire Forman Hardy family which owns the *Nottingham Evening Post* and has many other business interests, including printing works and the Kimberley Brewery. Colonel T. E. Forman Hardy, the proprietor, lists himself as a landowner, residing at his estate, Car Colston Hall, where his pedigree herds are raised.
   Although the *NFP* shows a concern for Sutton's own interests, it also takes much of its tone and picks up matters from its parent company based in Nottingham, fifteen miles away, which also distributes its free paper, the *Recorder*, in the area. The *NFP* is printed by the Huthwaite Printing Press in Sutton, a firm which also produces *Outlook*, the Thursday magazine for the *EP*, and is owned by T. Bailey Forman Ltd.

Chapter 6

1. Stewart Wilson (1980 B: 129).
2. Colin Fletcher (1978 A).
3. Tim Albert (1978).

Chapter 7

1. 'Schools in Britain today are under an intense barrage of criticism from the far right . . . [who argue that]
   (a) Children are not naturally good. This is the first line of Black Paper 1975 . . . added to this is the belief that modern schools are failing to cope with these "bad children" . . . public morality declines continually and all of our woes although based on the animal state of human nature are encouraged and abetted by our disfunctional schools . . .
   (b) In the "good old days" virtually everyone was literate and nearly everybody had respect for schools and intellectual rigour. There were stipulated standards; we had order, discipline, authority and traditional disciplines; there were unquestioned examination results and people "knew their place" . . .
   (c) Drill, repetition, practice, external motivation, class-teaching, corporal punishment and homework . . . Business-like training is an appropriate summary concept'—W. T. Lowe (1976: 8–9).
   These three points of reference, on human nature, on curriculum and on pedagogy, map the sources, tributaries and confluence of the new traditionalism. The head was challenged to reply in agreement and to respond in his every action accordingly.

Chapter 8

1. William T. Lowe (1976: 9).

Chapter 9

1. Paulo Freire recalls a person saying: 'When I began this course I was naive and when I found out how naive I was I started to get critical' (1972: 15).
2. Caroline Benn (1978: 9).
3. Christopher Price (1983: 72).

4. A. R. Delves and John Watts (1979: 27). See also Barry MacDonald (1978), David Hamilton *et al.* (1977).
5. *Times Education Supplement* editorial (1978).
6. As is the traditional concept of 'teacher identity' which holds that teachers may support reforms in schooling; or they may support developments in their own subject areas; or they may subscribe to professional values; or they may be active in one of the teachers unions. Each loyalty has weaknesses as well as strengths. Unionism, whilst creating collective strength and defending members from victimisation, also means that interest can be expressed mainly in terms of pay, conditions and contractual liabilities. The teacher may become a barrack-room lawyer who tells others how little they actually need to do. Professional identity likewise has strengths if it is taken to mean that the teacher acts and feels responsible for a class, but it can also imply an inherent superiority in relation to 'the clients'. The parents and the pupils can be seen as unfortunates and inferiors. Subject and specialist interests are similarly placed; their benefits are those of contemporary and forward-looking attitudes. Their weakness is a studied ignorance of the needs and value of similar developments taking place in other subjects and interest areas. Without an element of each of these loyalties, the teacher's identity in time is likely to reveal more weaknesses than strengths.
7. Terry Ellis *et al.* (1976: 141).
8. See Appendix II of the Auld Report (1976).
9. Caroline Benn (1978: 6–7).
10. See Whittaker *et al.* (1976: Chapter C).

References

Tim Albert (1978). 'Choking off Innovation: Sutton Centre', *New Statesman*, 17 March, p. 348.

Robin Auld (1976). *William Tyndale Junior and Infants School Public Enquiry: A Report to the Inner London Education Authority*, Inner London Education Authority.

Caroline Benn (1978). 'First They Came for the Socialists', *Socialism and Education*, Vol. 5, No. 6: 6–9.

Leila Berg (1968). *Risinghill: Death of a Comprehensive*, Penguin.

Gerald Birnbaum (1975). 'Countesthorpe College', in *Curriculum Innovation*, ed. A. Harris, M. Lawn and W. Prescott, Croom Helm, and edited from Gerald Birnbaum, *Case Studies of Educational Innovation: III At the School Level*, CERI/OECD, Paris, 1973.

Roger Dale (1979). 'The Politization of School Deviance: Reactions to William Tyndale', in *Schools, Pupils and Deviance*, ed. Len Barton and Roland Meighan, Nafferton: 95–112.

A. R. Delves and John Watts (1979). 'A Year of Education', *Forum*, Vol. 22, No. 1, p. 27–9.

Terry Ellis et al. (1976). *William Tyndale: The Teachers' Story*, Readers and Writers Cooperative.

Barry Elsey and Ken Thomas (1977). *School and Community*, School of Education, University of Nottingham.

Colin Fletcher (1978 A). 'A School on Trial', *New Society*, Vol. 43, No. 800, pp. 252–3.

— (1978 B). 'Assessing School Performance', *British Educational Research Journal*, Vol. 4, No. 2, pp. 51–61.

— (1980 A). 'The Sutton Centre Profile', in *Outcomes of Education*, ed. Tyrrel, Burgess and Elizabeth Adams, Macmillan: 46–55.

— (1980 B). 'A Community School' in *Schools, Teachers and Teaching*, ed. Len Barton and Stephen Walker, Falmer Press: 139–158.

— (1983). *The Challenges of Community Education: A Biography of Sutton Centre 1970–1983*, Department of Adult Education, University of Nottingham.

Paulo Freire (1972). *The Pedagogy of the Oppressed*, Penguin.

Harold Garfinkel (1967). *Studies in Ethnomethodology*, Prentice Hall.

Stuart Hall (1977). 'Education and the Crisis of the Urban School', in *The Urban School*, ed. John Raynor and Elizabeth Harris, Ward Lock Educational: 7–17.

Stuart Hall, Chas Cricher, Tony Jefferson, John Clarke, Brian Roberts (1978). *Policing the Crisis*, Macmillan.

David Hamilton *et al.* (1977). *Beyond the Numbers Game*, Macmillan.

David H. Hargreaves (1982). *The Challenge for the Comprehensive School, Culture, Curriculum and Community*, Routledge and Kegan Paul.

William T. Lowe (1976). 'Coping with Reactionary Criticism of Schools—Suggestions from the US Experience', *Forum*, Vol. 19, autumn, No. 1, pp. 8–11.

Barry MacDonald (1976). 'Evaluation and the Control of Education', in *Curriculum Evaluation Today: Trends and Implications*, ed. David Tawney, Macmillan: pp. 125–36.

— (1978). 'Accountability, Standards and Schooling', in *Accountability in Education*, ed. A. Becher and S. Maclure, National Foundation for Educational Research.

R. F. MacKenzie (1970). *State School*, Penguin, of which parts were originally published in *The Sins of the Children*, *Escape from the Classroom* and *A Question of Living*, all published by Collins.

— (1973). 'Teachers of the World Unite', in *Discipline in Schools*, ed. Barry Turner, Ward Lock Educational.

— (1977). *The Unbowed Head, Events at Summerhill Academy 1968–74*, Edinburgh University Student Publications Board.

Virginia Makins (1975; 1976). 'The Story of Countesthorpe', *The Times Educational Supplement*, 16 May 1975: reprinted in E203, *Curriculum Design and Development Case Study 5: Portrait of Countesthorpe College*, Item 3, The Open University 1976.

— (1978). 'A School Goes on Trial', *The Times Education Supplement*, No. 3265: 3.

Tim McMullen (1968). 'Flexibility for a Comprehensive School', *Forum*, Vol. 10, No. 2, pp. 64–7.

— (1972). 'Countesthorpe College', *Forum*, Vol. 14, No. 2, pp. 48–9.

— (1974). 'The Education of the Uninterested', W. B. Curry Lecture, October 1973, University of Exeter.

Mike Minchin (1975). *Countesthorpe College—problems and possibilities of radical innovation*, Dip. Ed. Thesis, University of Nottingham.

Open University (1976). E203, *Curriculum Design and Development Case Study 5: Portrait of Countesthorpe College*, Item 1 Countesthorpe: the Opening Year, Item 2 Countesthorpe: after Three Years, Item 3 Countesthorpe: after Five Years.

Christopher Price (1983). *The Times Educational Supplement*, No. 3517, 25, November 1983, p. 72.

David Reynolds and Michael Sullivan (1980). 'The Comprehensive Experience', in *Schools, Teachers and Teaching*, ed. Len Barton and Stephen Walker, Falmer Press: 121–38.

James Stone (1975). 'The Community Concept, 1 Nottinghamshire. Sutton brings school to the market place', *Education*, 145, 7 February, pp. 150–52.

George Taylor and John Saunders (1976). *Law of Education*, Butterworth.

Philip Toogood (1984). 'The Head's Tale', Dialogue Publications, Telford.

The Times Educational Supplement (1978). Editorial, 6 January 1978.

Willem van der Eyken and Barry Turner (1969). *Adventure in Education*, Penguin.

John Watts (1980). *Towards an Open School*, Longman.

— (ed.) (1977). *The Countesthorpe Experience*, Allen and Unwin.

— (1980 A). 'The Community College: Continuous Change', in *Issues in Community Education*, ed. Colin Fletcher and Neil Thompson, Falmer Press: 89–100.

C. Whittaker, P. Brown and J. Manahan (1976). *The Handbook of Environmental Powers*, Architectural Press.

Stewart Wilson (1980 A). 'Pen Portrait', in *Issues in Community Education*, ed. Colin Fletcher and Neil Thompson, Falmer Press: 203.

— (1980 B). 'The School and the Community', in *Issues in Community Education*, ed. Colin Fletcher and Neil Thompson, Falmer Press: 115–32.

— (1980 C). 'Eleventh Sessions at Sutton Centre as a Community Involvement', in *Issues in Community Education*, ed. Colin Fletcher and Neil Thompson, Falmer Press: 139–42.

Appendix

The Trial of William Tyndale School: events from the staff's account.
'one [person at the interview for headship] did not want him appointed' (p. 9).
'Before too long there was criticism of his failure to communicate with parents' (p. 19).
'All three, [the Head, the Chairman and Schools Inspector] were comparatively new to their jobs (p. 20).
'the Head set about establishing staff participation in decision making' (p. 11).
'At least one teacher was against this and complained directly to politicians and administrators' (p. 15).
'The latter quickly passed information to the press and up the political ladder' (p. 15).
'Managers were also in direct contact with parents' (p. 24).
'There were secret meetings' (p. 24).
' . . . and stories of great danger' (p. 22).
'Complaints were relayed as rumours' (p. 30).
' . . . and the scene widened with correspondence to national figures' (p. 29).
'A meeting of parents and governor/managers was highly charged' (p. 32).
'After that officials tried to keep the sides apart' (p. 36).
'Statements of staff aims were produced' (p. 50).
' . . . but the atmosphere was one of open conflict' (p. 38).
'The statements met with waves of more rumours' (p. 51).
'Alarming stories' (p. 56), 'and yet more special meetings' (p. 59), 'about which some of those who should have attended were not told' (p. 61).
'Some parents sought to quickly remove their children' (p. 65).
' . . . others rallied to support the staff' (p. 105).
'For a while it seemed that the conflict had lessened, but it had simply gone underground' (p. 62).

'Allegations were being collected, although the staff were not being told about them' (p. 80).

'The teachers were using the proper channels to County Hall and their trade unions' (p. 100).

'It seemed the authority had lost the initiative because two local government bodies were now also locked in conflict' (p. 87).

'The Education Authority did, however, announce that a full inspection would take place and this reasserted the Authority's power' (p. 107).

'The inspection would be used in an enquiry, although the details had not yet been worked out' (p. 125).

'The inspection came to represent the enquiry and vice versa' (p. 149).

Index